Anonymous

The Celebration of the Quarter-Millennial Anniversary of the Reformed Protestant Dutch Church

November 21st, 1878

Anonymous

The Celebration of the Quarter-Millennial Anniversary of the Reformed Protestant Dutch Church
November 21st, 1878

ISBN/EAN: 9783337296193

Printed in Europe, USA, Canada, Australia, Japan

Cover: Foto ©Lupo / pixelio.de

More available books at **www.hansebooks.com**

THE CELEBRATION

OF THE

ANNIVERSARY

OF THE

Reformed Protestant Dutch Church,

OF THE CITY OF NEW YORK.

Een-dracht maakt macht.

The Glory of Children are their Fathers.

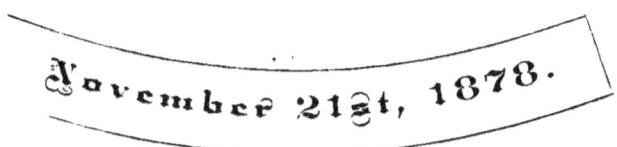

IN THE CHURCH, FIFTH AVENUE AND TWENTY-NINTH STREET.

1628—1878.

CONTENTS.

Prefatory Notice.

Services in the Afternoon:

Dr. Ormiston's Remarks.

Dr. Vermilye's Discourse.

Services in the Evening:

Address of the Rev. Dr. Dix.
Address of the Rev. Dr. Rogers.

Address of the Rev. Dr. Crosby.
Address of the Rev. Dr. Anderson.

Address of the Rev. Dr. Tiffany.
Address of the Rev. Dr. Storrs.

THE PROCEEDINGS.

At a meeting of the Consistory of the Reformed Protestant Dutch Church of the City of New York, held September 5th, 1878, the Rev. Dr. Chambers called attention to the fact, (of which he said that he had recently been reminded by the Rev. Dr. Corwin, of Millstone, N. J.), that the present year was the 250th since the organization of this church. The evidence of the fact is contained in the second volume of the "Documents relating to the Colonial History of the State of New York," published some years ago by order of the Legislature. The appendix to this volume gives at length a letter describing the first visit of an ordained minister to the Island of Manhattan. The letter was first printed about twenty years ago in the *Kerk-historisch Archief*, a periodical issued in Amsterdam, and in the year 1858 was translated and published in this country by the Hon. Henry C. Murphy, then minister at the Hague. It was addressed by the Rev. Jonas Michaelius to the Rev. Adrianus Smoutius, of Amsterdam. The writer had served as chaplain abroad in San Salvador and Guinea on the west coast of Africa, but in January, 1628, sailed to New Amsterdam, to labor under the superintendence of a committee of ministers appointed by the Synod of North Holland. The present letter is the first written after his arrival, and bears date August 11. In it, after an account of the voyage and its hardships, occurs the following passage:

"We have first established the form of a church (*gemeente*); and as Brother Bastiaen Crol very seldom comes down from Fort Orange, [Albany], because the directorship of that fort and the trade there is committed to him, it has been thought best to choose two elders for my assistance and for the proper consideration of all such ecclesiastical matters as might occur, intending the coming year, if the Lord permit, to let one of them retire and to choose another in his place from a double number first lawfully presented by the congregation. One of those whom we have chosen is the Honorable Director himself, and the other is the store-keeper of the Company, Jan Huyghen, his brother-in-law, persons of very good character as far as I have been able to learn; having both been formerly in office in the church, the one as deacon, the other as elder, in the Dutch and French churches respectively, at Wesel.

"We have had at the first administration of the Lord's Supper full fifty communicants—not without great joy and comfort for so many—Walloons and Dutch; of whom a portion made their first confession of faith before us, and others exhibited their church certificates. Others had forgotten to bring their certificates with them, not thinking that a church would be formed and established here; and some, who had brought them, had lost them unfortunately in a general conflagration, but they were admitted upon the satisfactory testimony of others to whom they were known and also upon their daily good deportment, since we cannot observe strictly all the usual formalities in making a beginning under such circumstances. We administer the Holy Sacrament of the Lord once in four months, provisionally until a larger number of people shall otherwise require. The Walloons and French have no service on Sunday, other than that in the Dutch language, of which they understand very little. Some of them live far away and could not come on account of the heavy rains and storms, so that it was neither advisable, nor was it possible, to appoint any special service for so small a number with so much uncertainty. Nevertheless, the Lord's Supper was administered to them in the French language, and according to the French mode, with a preceding discourse, which I had before me in writing, as I could not trust myself extemporaneously."

After the reading of this document, it was *"Resolved,* that this Consistory will observe the 250th anniversary of the origin and founding of this church, and that a committee of three be appointed to confer with the pastors and report on the time and manner of the celebration." Messrs. Theophilus A. Brouwer, James Anderson, M. D., and Henry Van Arsdale, M. D., were appointed the committee. At a subsequent meeting of the Consistory this committee reported, recommending that the celebration take place on the 21st of November, in the church on 29th Street and 5th Avenue, and suggesting such services as they considered appropriate to the occasion. The report was adopted, and the same committee was continued, with power to take charge of the anniversary and make the necessary provision for the exercises suggested. These were an historical discourse by the senior pastor in the afternoon, and a series of addresses of congratulation and sympathy in the evening, by representatives of the different denominations in our city, together with devotional services rendered by honored brethren of our own communion, the whole interspersed with suitable music. The committee accordingly made the requisite arrangements, issued invitations, prepared programmes and gave due notice, so that when the day arrived, although the weather was unfavorable, large audiences were in attendance, that of the evening being greater than the seating capacity of the church, and the entire plan was carried out, as shown by the reports herewith given, in a very gratifying way. At the next meeting of the Consistory (December 5) that body, by a formal vote, tendered their thanks to the committee "for the able and highly satisfactory manner in which they had discharged their duties."

The building in which the services were held was tastefully decorated for the occasion with flowers and banners. In the pulpit alcove, midway between floor and ceiling, was fastened a wreath of red and white roses encircling a white dove. A delicate festooned spray of ivy ran up above in graceful curves, meeting the edge of an American flag on the left and the edge of the Holland standard on the right. The flags swept down to the floor, and between them hung an anchor of white roses and pinks. The wall on each side was draped with American flags. The front of the preacher's stand was festooned with arbutus. A mass of white and yellow roses, pinks and carnations, in the centre of which in red flowers was worked the number "250," adorned the front of the desk. On the church wall, at the left of the pulpit, in the centre of a square frame of evergreens on a bank of white flowers, was worked "1628," and on the right, in a similar manner, "1878." Colored silk banners floated from the gallery rail, inscribed "Faith," "Hope," "Charity," "Obedience," "Love," "Genius," "Courage," "Mercy," &c. "Praise God from whom all blessings flow," was written over the organ pipes. The atmosphere of the church was redolent of the perfume of the flowers.

The music, under the direction of Dr. S. Austen Pearce and Mr. W. E. Beames, rendered by several combined choirs, numbering over seventy trained voices, aided by the organ and appropriate brass instruments, was of a very high order of merit.

Seats were reserved on the right hand of the pulpit for ruling elders and elders of the Great Consistory, and on the left for deacons in office and deacons of the Great Consistory. The officiating ministers occupied seats in the pulpit. They were followed from the vestry by Mayor Ely, Consul-General Burlage, from Holland; President De Peyster, of the New York Historical Society; President Monroe, of the Y. M. C. A.; Hon. John Jay, William E. Dodge, and other well-known residents of New York. Many members of the St. Nicholas and Historical Societies were among the congregation, and an unusually large number of clergymen, both of the Dutch Reformed Church and of all the other evangelical communions, occupied seats which had been reserved for them in the front of the church.

Present Officers of the Church.

Rev. THOMAS E. VERMILYE, D.D., LL.D., installed October 20, 1839.
Rev. TALBOT W. CHAMBERS, D.D., installed December 2, 1849.
Rev. WILLIAM ORMISTON, D.D., installed September 11, 1870.

Elders.

JAMES ANDERSON,
WILLIAM BOGARDUS,
THEOPHILUS A. BROUWER,
ROBERT BUCK,
PETER DONALD,
JOHN GRAHAM,

DANIEL P. INGRAHAM,
SAMUEL B. SCHIEFFELIN,
GAMALIEL G. SMITH,
JOHN L. SMITH,
HENRY VAN ARSDALE,
JOHN VAN NEST.

Deacons.

HENRY W. BOOKSTAVER,
WILLIAM L. BROWER,
JOHN S. BUSSING,
ROBERT DORSETT,
WILLIAM H. DUNNING,
JAMES S. FRANKLIN,

ALEXIS A. JULIEN,
HENRY E. KNOX,
NEILSON OLCOTT,
WILLIAM B. RUNK,
ABR'M V.W. VAN VECHTEN,
CHARLES H. WOODRUFF.

Clerk—GEORGE S. STITT, Esq.

Treasurer—JAMES PHYFE.

The Great Consistory.

RICHARD AMERMAN,
JAMES ANDERSON,
ABRAHAM BEEKMAN,
ABRAHAM BOGARDUS,
WILLIAM BOGARDUS,
ORLANDO M. BOGART,
HENRY W. BOOKSTAVER,
JAMES H. BRIGGS,
THEOPHILUS A. BROUWER,
WILLIAM L. BROWER,
ROBERT BUCK,
JOHN S. BUSSING,
CORNELIUS C. DEMAREST,
PETER DONALD,
ROBERT DORSETT,
WILLIAM H. DUNNING,
JAMES S. FRANKLIN,
WILLIAM C. GIFFING,
DAVID GILLESPIE,
JOHN GRAHAM,
STEPHEN HASBROUCK,
DANIEL HOWELL,
WILLIAM P. HOWELL,
DANIEL P. INGRAHAM,
GEORGE T. JACKSON,
PETER A. H. JACKSON,
ALEXIS A. JULIEN,
CALVIN E. KNOX,
HENRY E. KNOX,
JOHN LABAGH,
FREDERICK T. LOCKE,
FRANCIS T. LUQUEER,
EBENEZER MONROE,
ELBERT B. MONROE,
EDWARD A. MORRISON,
NEILSON OLCOTT,
JAMES PHYFE,
WILLIAM B. RUNK,
SAMUEL B. SCHIEFFELIN,
GAMALIEL G. SMITH,
GEORGE SMITH,
JOHN L. SMITH,
GEORGE S. STITT,
HENRY SNYDER,
HENRY VAN ARSDALE,
JAMES VAN BENSCHOTEN,
JOHN VAN NEST,
ABRAHAM V. W. VAN VECHTEN,
JASPER T. VAN VLECK,
CHARLES VAN WYCK,
EVERARDUS B. WARNER,
PETER R. WARNER,
WILLIAM WOOD,
CHARLES H. WOODRUFF,
JOHN S. WOODWARD,
WALLACE P. WILLETT.

Proceedings in the Afternoon.

These were conducted precisely in accordance with the following programme.

Programme for Afternoon Service.

Rev. William Ormiston, D.D., presiding.

1. **Doxology** { "Praise God from whom all blessings flow," } Tune, "Old Hundred"

2. **Anthem** — "O God, when Thou appearest." — Mozart

3. **Scripture Reading** by Rev. Wm. H. Campbell, D.D. { President of Rutgers College }

4. **Prayer** - - - by Rev. M. S. Hutton, D.D.

5. **Hymn 924** - - - - Tune, "St. Anns"

1. Our God, our help in ages past,
   Our hope for years to come,
   Our shelter from the stormy blast,
   And our eternal home :

2. Before the hills in order stood,
   Or earth received her frame,
   From everlasting Thou art God,
   To endless years the same.

3. Time, like an ever-rolling stream,
   Bears all its sons away;
   They fly, forgotten, as a dream
   Dies at the opening day.

4. Our God, our help in ages past,
   Our hope for years to come,
   Be Thou our guard while troubles last,
   And our eternal home !

Programme for Afternoon Service.

6 Historical Discourse by Rev. Thomas E. Vermilye, D.D.

7 Hymn 559 - - - Tune, "St. Thomas"

1. I love Thy kingdom, Lord,
   The house of Thine abode,
   The church our blest Redeemer saved
   With His own precious blood.

2. I love Thy church, O God!
   Her walls before Thee stand,
   Dear as the apple of Thine eye,
   And graven on Thy hand.

3. If e'er to bless Thy sons
   My voice or hands deny,
   These hands let useful skill forsake,
   This voice in silence die.

4. If e'er my heart forget
   Her welfare or her woe,
   Let every joy this heart forsake,
   And every grief o'erflow.

5. For her my tears shall fall,
   For her my prayers ascend;
   To her my cares and toils be given
   Till toils and cares shall end.

8 Hallelujah Chorus - - - Beethoven

9 Gloria Patri

10 Benediction by Rev. S. M. Woodbridge, D.D. { Of Theological Seminary, New Brunswick, N.J.

Music will be under the direction of Dr. S. Austen Pearce.

Mr. W. E. Beames will preside at Organ.

Afternoon Service.

At three o'clock the Rev. Dr. Ormiston took the chair, and after the appointed musical and devotional services had been rendered, made the following remarks introductory to the discourse of the occasion.

DR. ORMISTON'S REMARKS.

For a nation, church or family to commemorate marked events and special periods in their past history is as instinctively natural as it is eminently profitable. To recall with reverence and pride the moral worth, the noble deeds, and the heroic endurance of a devout, faithful and valorous ancestry is not more grateful than it is dutiful. Such an exercise is fitted to quicken piety, deepen gratitude, inspire patriotism, and stimulate to high and emulous endeavor.

Of late, in all parts of our land, centennial celebrations have been frequent and various, connected with events relating to the independence of the country and the formation of its government. Doubtless these services have availed much in deepening the sentiments of patriotism and reverence in the hearts of the people.

Many churches, also, have taken a retrospective survey of their origin and progress, with a view to fresher effort for greater achievements in the future.

This is the purpose of our assembly to-day. We

propose reverently and gratefully to refer to the organization and history of a congregation whose origin is coeval with the first settlement of the country, and antedates the founding of our city. It is probably the only Protestant church organization in the United States which has attained its two hundred and fiftieth year.

Shortly after the exploration of the Hudson by the adventurous navigator whose name it bears, emigrants from Holland, then a powerful state and the home of civil and religious liberty, came to the Island of Manhattan and the banks of the Hudson for purposes of trade. They brought with them an open Bible and religious ordinances, and were the first evangelists in the state.

Their interesting story will be eloquently told by my revered colleague, the senior pastor of the church, to whom, with great propriety, that duty has been assigned.

I would only further say, that, without detracting in the slightest degree from the merits and services of other early settlers and churches, we may, with perfect sincerity and becoming modesty, claim, for our Dutch forefathers, a prominent place in establishing the civil and religious institutions of this republic.

The Reformed Protestant Church of the Netherlands, whence they came, was characterized by a sound scriptural orthodoxy and a liberal, enlightened charity. Steadfast in principle and catholic in spirit, her relations with the churches of Great Britain were intimate and friendly. The persecuted of other countries sought a refuge in that land and received a cordial welcome from the church. Freedom of conscience was the common privilege of all—citizen and stranger alike. The Pilgrim Fathers themselves, whose frequent eulogiums are well merited, found there a home, and a school where they learned much concerning the management of both civil and ecclesiastical affairs, which greatly affected their views and policy in moulding the institutions of the new world where they found a permanent home.

We may be honestly proud of the founders and fathers of our venerable church. Faithful in their adherence to scriptural doctrine and the rights of conscience—insisting on an educated ministry for the church and good common schools for the children—staunch and dauntless in the maintenance of civil freedom and free institutions—industrious, frugal and home-loving in their habits, they were fit founders of the institutions of a new land, and worthy ancestors of a free, God-fearing posterity. Directly and indirectly we owe them much, and we lovingly revere their memory.

Nor would I claim too much were I to say that, though we may differ from our honored ancestors in many things, yet as a church we still retain the same love for the truth of God, and the same zeal for its maintenance, defence and extension; and sustain towards all other evangelical churches the same loving, brotherly regards.

Holding the same system of doctrine—maintaining the same ecclesiastical polity—observing the same customs with but little variation, and evincing the same spirit of christian catholicity, the Reformed Church of to-day exhibits many lineaments which unmistakably indicate her hereditary family likeness. Cherishing tenaciously her own time-honored customs, she profoundly respects the conscientious convictions and established practices of all sister churches, with whom she seeks to live in the unity of the Spirit, as children of the same Father, and servants of the same King. May our precious heritage be the inheritance of our children.

DR. VERMILYE'S DISCOURSE.

PRELIMINARY REMARKS.

The speaker prefaced the address with the following remarks: "I have received many visits, and a number of letters from various quarters, which show the profound interest everywhere taken in this anniversary. One of these is from a lady in Philadelphia, whose possession of the time-honored prefix 'Van,' vouches for her right to send a letter of congratulation. I have also here a copy of the charter, granted by William III, in 1696, to 'the minister, elders and deacons of the Reformed Protestant Dutch Church of the City of New York.' Among the incorporators are names still found among us—William Beekman and Jacob Kip.

"I hold in my hand—(Dr. V. exhibited a handsome gold-headed cane)—an interesting memorial, presented in commemoration of this occasion by one who is a Van of the Vans. It is made of a piece of the wood used in the construction of the old North Church in William Street, recently taken down, and within the top is placed a thimbleful of the soil of the Netherlands mingled with a little earth taken from the spot where the first Dutch Church on this continent was planted, thus aptly symbolizing, as the donor happily expresses it, the union of the two countries in the commingling of their soils. Upon the head is engraved the name of Dr. Vermilye, and upon the sides those of Drs. Chambers and Ormiston, with the years 1628, 1728. I shall keep it and prize it dearly till I die."

DISCOURSE.

We meet by the invitation of "The Consistory of the Reformed Protestant Dutch Church of the City of New York," to commemorate the 250th Anniversary of its existence—the Mother of the Dutch Churches in this City, and, in a sense, of the entire denomination: of regularly organized churches the eldest, we believe, of the Protestant family on the continent: the forerunner, commissioned like the Baptist in the wilderness, to herald on the shores of the newly discovered world the sublime command, "Prepare ye the way of the Lord: make straight in the desert a highway for our God." The occasion appeals naturally to the sympathies, not of the people of this particular congregation or of our communion only, but to the descendants of the Dutch wherever and in whatever religious connexion they may be found; to our fellow christians of every name; no less to the student of history, the man of letters, the patriot who is interested in the development of the state; to every one who intelligently notes the march of events, and hopes and believes in human advancement. The Consistory has assigned to me the duty and the honor of giving the commemorative discourse. And without delaying upon the "*exordium remotum*" of our ancient form, and without formal approach by rhetorical preliminaries, I pass at once to the subject before us.

Of the people who early settled this continent from the various parts of Europe, two, or rather three, nationalities were especially present. And these, let it be marked, were the most advanced in civil liberty, and the most determined defenders of the Protestant faith: the English, who first settled Virginia, but afterwards were more largely represented by the Puritans of New England; and the Dutch, who founded Manhattan, spread along the Hudson as far as Albany, west into New Jersey and down upon the Delaware. With subsequent immigrations came the Huguenots in considerable numbers, flying from the fiery persecutions in France. And, although companies of them located in Maine and Massachusetts, where their names and some interesting relics still exist; and others found a home in and about Charleston, South Carolina, and are yet represented there by worthy descendants — the largest portion established themselves in this region. Their social and flexible character caused them easily to assimilate and become one with the Dutch, while they in turn exerted a very happy influence upon the people with whom they mingled; and to this day, places and families among the most noted and honored in the land, bearing Huguenot names, attest the excellent quality of that element in the formation of our social, and religious, and political life.

But from Holland came the founders of our City and State: "our Alban Fathers and the walls of lofty Rome." It is a singular territory. There, man, under the most unpropitious conditions, in the words of the poet, has "scooped out an empire and usurped the shore." It lies on the border of the sea—almost *in* the sea—opposite the south-east coast of England; and has been formed evidently by the detritus of the rivers, the Rhine especially, brought down even from the high Alps, and by the sand thrown up from the abyss of the ocean; originally a morass, which the tide overflowed, and which no sagacity could have predicted would become dry land fit to be inhabited; the accretions of ages and persistent skill have brought it forth. The rivers have flowed on and left their deposits; the ocean has piled up the sand for soil, and pebbles and stones which formed the downs; and by vast labors of man they have become a solid bulwark against the farther encroachment of the waters, securing a safe and commodious habitation. Many parts lie much below the level of the sea, protected from inundation only by the dykes. And it was very exciting in riding through the beautiful park at

Rotterdam, to pass along the base of this wall and see seagoing steamers and ships, of the largest bulk, at anchor apparently more than a hundred feet directly above us. The dyke was the only protection. And as I gazed, I realized the grandeur of the divine interdict, " Hitherto shalt thou come and no farther: and here shall thy proud waves be stayed." Much of the soil thus recovered from the sea, with incredible toil and cost, would be thought too poor to recompense the husbandman. But the patient industry of a free people, expended upon it for centuries, has made it productive almost beyond imagination. And those parts recovered directly from the ocean, and at first but sand, were made among the most productive of all. Everywhere rich vegetation appeared. Populous and thriving cities grew up like lodges in a garden of delights. The canals also, so readily constructed and supplied with water, became an easy means of internal communication; like the blood vessels of the human system conveying life and vigor throughout the corporate body.

But besides its agricultural character, and perhaps almost by a natural necessity, from its proximity to the sea, Holland became a maritime power. Its hardy sons were trained to face the storms and breast the billows of every ocean, and bring home the treasures of "the gorgeous East and the opening West." Thus by the operation of natural causes and the persistent labor of an energetic race was the country gradually prepared for a high destiny. Small in size—scarcely appearing upon the geographical map of Europe—and most unpromising at the beginning, instead of remaining a sterile and desolate shore, where only the fisherman spread his nets, it has supported in abundance and happiness a greater number of people in proportion to its area, than any other country on the globe. Other lands needed but to be cleared for occupation—this to be created. Its existence shows how intelligent, untiring industry, against almost insuperable difficulties, can make "the desert blossom like the rose." As its history will likewise teach us what man himself may become under the pressure of great and urgent necessities. I am reminded of a pleasant anecdote told by the late Hermanus Bleecker. When he was minister near the Hague, he was accompanied on one occasion by a gentleman of high position, to the top of the main church in Amsterdam, from which one might take in at one view almost the entire seven provinces. As they looked around, the gentleman exclaimed with great animation and pardonable pride, "we are a small territory, Mr. Bleecker, but we are a great people."

And in truth their history is even more remarkable than the physical characteristics of the country. As far back as authentic records penetrate, the people of the Low Countries, *i. e.* of the northern provinces, which we intend when we speak of Holland, as distinguished from the Highlands, to which the country rises from the sea on the east and the south, and whose inhabitants were originally from a different stock and have always showed somewhat different traits—from the earliest annals the people of the lowlands have borne one character: simple, frugal, honest, patient of toil; intelligent rather than imaginative; not propense to war, yet indomitably bold, full of endurance, and prompt to maintain their liberty and rights. Their local situation would seem to indicate that the peaceable occupations of agriculture and commerce were their natural destiny. Enterprise would be expended in trade for the acquisition of wealth rather than in the pursuit of military renown, the extension of territory, or the enlargement of power. Yet no country in Europe has been so often the theatre of sanguinary wars—not of her own seeking, but in defense of her soil; or, as the convenient battle ground of her neighbors where their common liberty was vindicated. And their endurance and successes are the astonishment of the world. It would seem as if an invading army might march over the level land almost without resistance. But Cæsar's trained legions were boldly met and checked by the intrepid Belgæ. For eighty years the conflict was prolonged with Spain, the strongest power in Europe. There William of Orange, in the spirit of his memorable motto: "*I will maintain; I will hold on;*" now beaten, and then victorious, kept the French at bay; and Marlborough succeeding him, at length foiled their best armies until the Grand Monarque was ruined by the struggle. They had conquered the land from the ocean; they held it against all comers. And Holland achieved the glory of a nation of heroes; as by her commerce she subsidized the east and the west, gathered their wealth into her treasury and became the richest people in the world. So was it with the Queen of the Adriatic. And in many respects the history of these two most singular countries is not dissimilar.

But Holland was not merely a field of arms, or a nation of traders. She became also the chosen seat of learning. The education of the young was carefully regarded. An evidence of a very interesting character survives in the school of our church, still flourishing as ever, under Mr. Dunshee, its able principal; the first literary institution probably in the country; established in 1626, and the teachers brought from Holland at that early date. It proves the value the Dutch placed on right education. Their universities, Utrecht and Leyden especially, were among the foremost in a learned age. Men of renown filled the professorial chairs, and students came from all parts. The founding of the university at Leyden rises to moral sublimity. When, by the unconquerable boldness of her sons, the tide of Spanish invasion had been rolled away, the Prince of Orange, in remembrance and acknowledgment of their deeds, offered to make Leyden the seat of an annual fair which would bring wealth to the city, or of a university: and the citizens grandly chose the University. There it has stood and stands—the monument of the great struggle and of the heroism of their fathers; but still more the monument of their nobility of thought; perpetuating their intellectual and moral life: the life of culture, of progress, of power, of a free people, which the blood of the sires purchased for their sons. Few things are so impressive as to stand, as I have done more than once, in its council chamber, and recall its origin, and look upon the portraits of scholars and statesmen, orators and soldiers, whose names are the glory of their own land, and whose figures stand boldly out upon the historic canvass of the great men of all times.

The invention of printing, the art of arts, contested by several and especially by Gutenberg, of Mentz, belongs almost demonstrably to Koster, of Haarlem, about 1438; although improved and perfected, it may be, by Gutenberg, from models secretly conveyed, it is said, from Koster.

And it is worthy of note, that the Latin Vulgate was probably the first complete printed volume, done by Gutenberg, at Mentz, about 1455. In Holland, the press was free from censorship, which continued in England as late as 1694 so that authors interdicted there printed their books abroad. Tyndale's translation, 1535, not allowed to be printed in England, was thus printed abroad and carried back and secretly distributed at home. Thus Germany and Holland deserve the credit, beyond their age, of just and advanced thought and corresponding action, in this great means of public enlightenment and progress; and by its liberal course, Holland, in its full measure, became the printing and publishing house of Europe; much to its own advantage as well as that of letters. Milton would there have found no cause to fulminate his grand, indignant sentences, to the men of the great commonwealth, on unlicensed printing; and Locke, as late as 1694, would have had no call to utter protests on the same subject, happily, the last protests needed in free and enlightened England.

From such causes and the toleration there existing, scholars as well as persecuted religionists, and even political refugees, long found a safe and quiet asylum in the Low Countries. Burnet and Locke, with others, driven from England, took shelter there and freely pursued their studies. These latter remarks apply, however, most strictly to the times when and after the Republic was inaugurated. The period of her greatness was one of those epochs in which mind seems to be uncommonly active, and all the wheels of life roll on with uncommon energy. From 1500, onwards, for nearly two centuries, Holland performed the most illustrious part on the theatre of events. She seemed the pivot on which Europe moved. It was the time of her greatest sufferings, and of her meridian splendor. She was the mainspring and seat of political negotiations; the arena of battles; the mediator of peace; the retreat of the persecuted for conscience sake from other lands; the strength of the weak, and the light-bearer of the times. Her statesmen read law to the nations; her warriors fought the battles of freedom and shattered the arm of arbitrary power; her scholars instructed the mind of the age; her divines expounded the faith by which Protestantism yet lives. We give this as a true description of Holland's place and influence in the time of her maturity; and from this land of wonders, from such a stock, at just about the culminating point of this great social and national development, came the discoverers and first settlers of Manhattan.

The juncture of time was of most auspicious omen. In the year 1609, the long conflict with Spain was suspended at the suggestion of Philip III, by a truce for twelve years. The indomitable Dutch were reluctant to accept it, so little did they bend under their burden—so warlike had they become. For during the whole continuance of the struggle they were carrying on their commerce and actually augmenting their strength. The truce was in reality a confession on the part of Spain that she was vanquished, and practically established the independence of the United Netherlands. Henceforth, Holland was acknowledged among nations as a free, self-governing Republic. It was in the very same year that Hudson sailed on the voyage which resulted in the discovery of the river that bears his name, which he explored to Albany; and in the acquisition by Holland of the vast region extending from the Capes of Delaware to Canada, styled the New Netherlands. True, discoveries had already been made by the English in Virginia; the Huguenots in Florida; the French in Acadia, now Canada. But the wide region I have mentioned was yet unknown. The Dutch explored Long Island Sound and discovered the Housatonic and Connecticut rivers, and rightly claimed the adjoining territory which the English wrested from them; nor were content until they had gorged New Amsterdam also. The admirable adaptation of this island as a mart of trade with the natives, and of the harbor for commerce was quickly understood. In 1614, the New Netherlands Company was chartered for four years, and made Manhattan a trading port. In 1621, the West India Company was formed to conduct commerce in the west, and Manhattan came under their power in fee. And it should never be forgotten that the island first held by discovery and occupancy, the right of might, was in 1621 fairly purchased from the natives, thus admitting their ownership, for twenty-four dollars.*

The West India Company appointed its own governors of the island, and of course its affairs were conducted on Dutch principles, as well as by Dutch men. The principles were integrity and strict honor; the men righteous and often dogmatical governors.

Hitherto I have not spoken of RELIGION. It was not to be imagined that a people so reflective and earnest should be indifferent on such a subject either at home or in their colonies. Always their national life had been invigorated by religious faith. When, then, the Reformation arose, it was a thing of course that the new movement, which upheaved the foundations of society in the nations around, should at once awaken deep interest and sympathy in Holland, and that the simplicity of form and purity of doctrine of the new teachers, when once understood, should be preferred by very many to the corrupt teachings and elaborate and sensuous ceremonial of Popery. And they had the charm of novelty. But there was a special cause which, beyond question, had great influence in confirming this feeling. The nation with which they

---

* Our honored president of the Historical Society has made a curious calculation that by this time, computing interest, the $24 would reach a sum almost beyond the power of figures. It brings to mind an incident in the early history of Massachussetts, when a large portion of the town of West Springfield, one of the most beautiful parts of the Connecticut river, was "*swapped*" for a wheelbarrow. What that barrow would be worth at this time *(in fiat money)* I cannot say. But it should be an Alpine heap.

warred, their cruel and relentless oppressor, was Catholic: who forbade all freedom of action and even of thought upon religious subjects; who had pursued them in ferocious war on that account; whose determined purpose it had been for eighty years to force Popery upon them with its hellish inquisition, its servility and chains. They had resisted unto blood in maintaining the better part; and it had the power over them of dearly purchased right. The system they chose, however, was not derived from Germany, as might have been expected, but from France or Geneva. They became Calvinists and Presbyterians—not Lutherans—and that was the form they introduced into the colony. The precise time of planting the church here was also significant. It was not only at the period of Holland's supremacy, in social elegance, in learning, in jurisprudence and politics; but it was during the agitations attendant upon and succeeding the sitting of the celebrated Synod of Dort: a fact which very discernably exerted an influence upon the church of the colony, as it did upon all the interests of church and state at home. Of that famous Synod let us then say a few words. It was convoked by the States General; was composed of delegates from the several provinces; and from the foreign churches; the Church of England included, and only the French Reformed absent, by the interdict of their king. It met at Dort on the 13th of November, 1618, and was called to consider and settle the theological controversy which arose from the teachings of James Arminius, professor of theology at Leyden, which were opposed by Francis Gomarus, likewise professor. Hence the parties were designated as Arminians and Gomarists; but from a remonstrance presented by the minority, they were also more generally known as remonstrants, who were the Arminians, and contra-remonstrants, who were Gomarists or Calvinists—and certainly of the straighter sort. It was substantially the old controversy of Augustine and Pelagius, and later of the Semi-Pelagians. It was before Augustine; for of such controversies, whether of form or substance, it may be truly said, there is nothing new under the sun; nor was it finally disposed of in his time. And although the points in issue were thoroughly discussed at Dort, it was not then terminated; and we may predict it never will be to the universal agreement of minds that think, as free minds will think, from different positions upon different lines. The more imperative the reason for tolerance and charity. The Synod held 152 sessions, and was dissolved in May, 1619: the president declaring that " its miraculous labors had made hell tremble ; " a prominent member saying that in that Synod "there were some things divine; some things human; and some things diabolical." The proportions however not precisely stated. Anterior to the meeting of the Synod the matters in dispute had convulsed the universities and churches and families, and involved the peace of the state. Nor did the decisions of the Synod which were on the side of the Calvinists, they being the majority, allay the storm. Alas! that such dire effects should flow from such causes. Yet this is human nature. And all history teaches that the wildest excitements and the fiercest wars, have sprung up on just such apparently inappropriate grounds. I do not think that they who most cordially adopt the theological conclusions of the Synod are bound, at this day, to defend the spirit which, for a large part, animated its leaders. In many of their utterances and deeds they manifested anything but christian meekness and were vindictive and cruel. But private interests became deeply implicated, and passions were embittered and furious. And, in judging the case, candor bids us remember that Calvinism was the long settled creed of Holland—that the Arminians were the aggressors—that in the pulpits and even in the theological chairs they persisted, contrary to earnest expostulation in teaching doctrines which the Calvinists sincerely believed not only to be contrary to the standards, but subversive of the faith delivered to the saints. And the experience they had had in the Catholic church, showed them the power of ideas to corrupt; made them more intense in their beliefs; and warned them against principles which they imagined led by logical sequence, to some of the worst errors of Rome. They may have been wrong, but, no doubt, they were sincere. The question involved is a very plain one. It is not whether men shall teach and act according to their convictions, but whether it is honest and to be tolerated, that they shall use the advantages of position and emoluments they have received on specific conditions, to undermine and overthrow sentiments and institutions they solemnly pledged themselves to uphold. And he has read very superficially, who has not learned that heresiarchs, while unchallenged, easily to their own satisfaction reconcile their defections from the old paths with rectitude; particularly if their interests are concerned. Sometimes, no doubt, it is because they do not fairly realize how far they have deflected from the right line; but oftener, probably, because self-opinion stands for divine illumination, and they imagine they have been elected by supernal wisdom to pour light upon the darkness of all preceding ages. That one's convictions run counter to the principles or practices of an association is a very good reason why he should not enter or should leave it; but a very bad reason that he should enter or remain in bad faith to subvert what he is appointed to defend. Arminians are apt to look only on their side, and then the Synod of Dort was an unparalleled atrocity, and its theology necessarily unsound. So, a class of religionists seem to see on the long, dark page of martyrology, but one sentence: "Calvin burned Servetus." That easy but false formula, they would have us think, refutes Calvinism, and demonstrates Socinianism. Happily a brighter light has dawned or a better spirit has come to our times— not we would hope from mere laxness of conviction but a widening of intelligence and love—and a rigid Calvinist may now believe, without incurring the penalty, *de haeretico comburendo*, that an Arminian can be saved.

But that Synod was not all polemical and diabolical. Many measures were adopted for the advancement of practical religion, having no connexion with controversy. A new translation of the Bible was likewise directed: a work begun on the order of the States by S. Aldegonde as early as 1594, and discontinued at his death. Six eminent scholars were

appointed as translators, and six substitutes, in case of the
failure of the translators, of whom two died during the progress
of the work. A company of final revisers was also appointed;
all most approved scholars. The translators and their families
were collected at Leyden, and supported at the public expense;
and after the most careful elaboration, the work was finished
and printed in 1637, at a cost to the States General of twenty-
five thousand pounds sterling, and ordered to be used in the
churches. The translation has been as highly prized by the
Dutch, as our English version, which came into use about
the same time, has been cherished by the English speaking
race; and the notes and comments of the translators, also published, are held in high estimation by Biblical scholars.

I may be excused for having enlarged upon this Synod,
for it supplied the theological life-blood of the Dutch church,
which yet has not all run out.

Although the advent of the colonists to Manhattan was
in those troublous times, they were not fugitives, as were the
Huguenots, from Popish, or the Puritans from Protestant
persecution. They belonged to the ruling party in the Mother
Country, and brought with them, as a thing of course, the
established church order and the Calvinistic creed, and somewhat perhaps of the spirit of the contra-remonstrants. And
that creed, symbolized in the *Heidelberg Catechism*, adopted
at a Synod of Dort as early as 1574, and re-affirmed by the
celebrated Synod in 1619, has ever prevailed in the Dutch
churches in this country. As the Synod stamped it with the
seal of orthodoxy, the immigrants held it fast as living truth;
the more that great and holy men had so strenuously con-
tended for it at home. This will account, in measure at least,
for the steady adherence of the Dutch church among ourselves
to its doctrines while conceding to others full liberty in their
own communions. Just as in Holland all fugitives found a
refuge; but she would tolerate no faithlessness in her own
church.

Wise policy as well as just principle directed the West
India Company to supply their trading posts and colonies with

the means of education and religion—and such provision, we are assured, from the first was made for Manhattan. We know that in 1626 two pious school masters came over with Director Minuet. Their duty, besides instructing the youth in secular learning, was to conduct religious services on the sabbath day, by reading the Scriptures, the creed and a sermon; (much like the deacons' meetings in New England); and they were to minister to the sick until such time as an ordained minister should be provided. From the latter duty they were called "*Zicken-troosters*," *i. e.* Comforters of the sick. Until recently, it was thought that the first ordained minister was the Reverend Everardus Bogardus, who came with Governor Wouter Van Twiller in 1633; and that he organized the church in that year. But a letter discovered by Mr. Murphy when he was minister at the Hague, written by the Rev. Jonas Michaelius, says, he "arrived at the Island of Manhattan the 11th of August, 1628;" and adds: "we first established the form of a church; and it has been thought best to choose two elders for my assistance; one of them is the Hon. Director himself. We had at the first administration of the Lord's supper full fifty communicants—Walloons and Dutch." This was five years before the arrival of Dominie Bogardus; and fixes the origin of the church in 1628; which date will make the Dutch, the oldest organized Protestant church in the New World. At least I am not aware of any earlier regular organized body. And the primitive organization lives in the collegiate church—" whose were the fathers"— which retains the title; the charter; the unbroken succession of the ministry and consistory; the records from the beginning; and the property from time to time bequeathed to the " Reformed Protestant Dutch Church of the City of New York" —at least so much as remains. Of these funds a liberal use has always been made by the consistory for the benefit of other churches and for objects of general utility to the denomination. I think I am justified in saying that, excepting for the building of their church edifices, a very liberal proportion, compared with their own expenditures, has been thus dispensed in past times to their brethren. Whether such aid does not often injure, by impairing the feeling of self-reliance, is a serious doubt.

The ruling power of each Dutch church is in the consistory—for it is Presbyterian and representative, and not Congregational. The ministers, elders and deacons, compose the consistory: the minister, according to apostolical commission, to preach, administer ordinances and exercise the pastoral supervision; the elders to assist him in spiritual matters, but not to preach or administer the sacraments; the deacons, as at the first, to attend to the poor and serve tables. Thus we see in each church a regular order. From the letter of Michaelius we learn that he ordained two elders. Necessarily that organization was imperfect. But as the church grew in numbers, it at length assumed its normal form of consistories, classes, particular and general Synods—a complete system for the denomination—and thus it is at present constituted. According to the ancient rules, to the consistories pertained the control of temporal as well as spiritual matters, as now in most of our churches. But several years ago, in courtesy to the popular craving for a share of whatever office or power may exist, authority was granted by legislative enactments in this State, to commit the temporalities to a Board of Trustees, elected by the pew-holders. This practice has been adopted in some of our churches, but is by no means generally accepted. A peculiarity of Dutch, as compared with Scotch or Irish Presbyterianism, is the rotation of the lay members of consistory. Their election for two years, instead of for life, although eligible to re-election, is thought to possess these advantages: that a larger number of the male members may become interested in the affairs of their church, and thus a Board of Trustees is superfluous; and also, that a troublesome or unqualified member may be quietly dropped—a great blessing often to pastors, consistories and people.

Our church, both here and in the Mother Country, has always demanded an educated ministry, and has shown no inclination to be long satisfied with sound for substance, ranting for reason, or professions for piety. The first preachers were men of solid parts, imbued with the excellent learning that at that day abounded in Holland. It was long the custom and for a time a necessity for the churches in the colony, not only to obtain their ministers from the Mother Country, but, also, to send thither young men of promise, desiring the ministry, to be educated and ordained. Utrecht and Leyden received such from all parts. Alas! how changed! Three years ago, when at Leyden, a learned professor informed me that of the 800 students, but eight were pursuing theology. And, with a meaning glance, he was at the pains to tell me that the theologues were the stoutest Darwinians in the University. If so, the fewer their numbers the better. At Utrecht there were somewhat more. Heidelberg had about the same small number. And from good authority I learned that reverence for the inspired word was much diminished by the influence of modern ideas, called science, and that personal religion seemed at a low ebb. Dr. Livingston settled here in 1770, more than 150 years after Manhattan was founded, having spent four years at Utrecht, in preparation for his work. He was one of the last, or the last, so educated, and brought the Holland mode of preaching by logical, orderly, but, perhaps, too precise and numerous divisions; and when made professor at New Brunswick, he used the Holland style of theological tuition—the much spoken of "*Classis argumentorum;*" systematic, thorough as far as it went; dry as a bone, but really teaching theology, and vastly to be preferred to a hap-hazard method that teaches nothing. The Dutch descent and Dutch training of Dr. Livingston, no doubt, conduced very largely to his popularity among his people. He occasionally preached in that language for the comfort of some of the aged; but Dr. Kuypers was the last who did so. The connexion of New Amsterdam, as it was then named, with Holland, had much relaxed after it passed under English sway in 1664 and became New York. Many returned home and few came. Intercourse was much with England; little with Holland. The colony was estranged, though not alienated. And while at the transfer, all the rights of the

Dutch church were secured by treaty, and the language continued in use in social life and in religious services, yet English being that of the ruling class, of course, encroached upon and gradually supplanted the Dutch. Hence, arose the strife, chiefly between the young and the old people, in regard to a change to English preaching; which, when yielded and determined by the calling of Dr. Laidley in 1764, just one hundred years from the English occupation, sent off a large portion of the opponents of English preaching with true Dutch spunk and admirable consistency to the English church. In like manner, the foreign education of the ministry and dependence of the churches upon the classis of Amsterdam, led to the *Cœtus* and *Conferentie* controversy, which resulted in the final independence of the American churches and ministry, and in the establishment of our own Classes, and of the Institution at New Brunswick. It was not strange that the Dutch language and customs declined: rather it was perfectly characteristic and highly creditable to the steady people, that their attachment to Holland, its language and whatever was Dutch should have lingered among them so long, under such adverse circumstances. Yet, natural as it was, no one can now doubt, that the pertinacity it assumed at several junctures, was injurious to the church; as there can be as little doubt that a too facile yielding to innovations in more recent times, has been equally disastrous.

The pastors of the Collegiate church have always been on an equality, excepting the deference which christian and gentlemanly courtesy has yielded to the senior. Until quite lately they performed in rotation the same services in all the churches. They wore, and continue to wear, the Geneva gown and bands, in which costume they were accustomed to walk from their dwellings to the church on the sabbath-day. As that practice might now be thought to savor of ostentation, it is discontinued, and the ministers are robed in the vestry. With the portraits of the ministers the walls of the consistory chamber are adorned; I say *adorned;* for really they form a comely and intellectual-featured gallery, not speaking of the living.

The public worship was arranged of course in conformity with that of the mother church. The order became a part of the constitution, and was made obligatory, so as to secure a proper uniformity throughout the denomination, and was not left to the taste, or want of taste, or caprice of individual ministers or congregations, which destroys the similitude of the service and ensures disorder. There was sufficient form to engage reverential attention and not allow religion to be stripped bare; yet there was not so much formality that it became perfunctory and exhausted devotion in rites and ceremonies. The psalmody was also fixed by law. In church the elders sat in the pew on the right, the deacons on the left of the pulpit. At the close of the service, when the minister descended, they stood to receive him, and each gave the right hand of fellowship and approval. The clerk, in his desk beneath the pulpit, opened the morning service by reading the commandments and announcing the psalm to be sung, when the organ pealed forth and the whole congregation united in praise. And never, I think, in Spurgeon's tabernacle in London, nor in the great churches in Holland, have I heard such impressive congregational singing as when Mr. Earle led and the vast assemblage joined in the old Middle Church, or Mr. Sage in the North. While singing the minister entered, stood for a few moments reverently at the foot of the pulpit stairs in silent prayer, his back to the people, ascended the pulpit and conducted the service. Preceding the second, or long prayer as it is sometimes termed, came the salutation, reading the S. S. and the "*exordium remotum*"—an address having, as the name expressed, a remote, and often a very remote, bearing on the subject of the sermon. In the old churches tablets were hung upon the walls, indicating the psalm to be read or sung.*

---

*Over the pulpit, in the North Church, hung the Harpendinck coat of arms, as it was thought to be; but perhaps, as Dr. DeWitt reasonably thinks, a memorial, placed there by the Consistory, in remembrance of the donation of his farm to the Consistory—a large tract of land, then a pasturage, now occupied by stores—from which has come the most of the property of the Collegiate Church. The motto would seem to confirm this idea: "*Dando Conservat*" "by giving, he keeps."

This was the order still observed in my youth in the old Middle and North Churches, so that when in Holland, although I understood nothing of the language, the service was not strange. And at Haarlem the crowd that collected at the cathedral evening service brought vividly to my mind the great congregation which, on sabbath evenings, used to fill the old Middle Church with people gathered from the various churches around.

On baptismal and communion occasions the entire forms were always read. The mother presented the child; and at the Lord's Supper the participants sat at tables spread through the aisles, filled frequently three or four times; and as addresses were made at each table the service was often greatly protracted. It was also the usage of the Dutch church to observe the days of special religious memorial: as Christmas, Easter, and those commonly observed by the Protestant communities in Europe. Nor did they feel that by thus emphasizing the great facts of Christianity they were guilty of any obsequious and irreligious imitation of mystic Babylon.

From the first it was required of the ministers that on the Lord's day afternoon they should expound the *Heidelberg Catechism;* going through it once every year. In time this custom naturally became repetitious and formal, and lost very much of its interest with the people; and a change was ordained by constitutional authority. When the old Middle Church was being dismantled and converted into a post-office, Dr. Knox, of sacred and beloved memory, and I, there met good Dr. Milner. As we stood in the pulpit, looking on the ruin, and recalling the days of old, the years of many generations of worshippers in the venerable edifice, Dr. Milner said: " do you keep up the custom of preaching on the catechism every Sunday afternoon?" "No, Sir;" replied Dr. Knox, in his mild tone; "it has been directed that we shall go through it once in four years instead of one." " That is," retorted Dr. Milner very pleasantly, "you are obliged to make it four times as tedious as before." Yet while the pleasantry was relished, and the former custom might have been irksome and a change might have become desirable, it seems a simple dictate of reason and prudence, that some method should be adopted in all churches by which the people may receive distinct and systematic instruction in the evidences and articles of their faith. Never, probably, was careful elementary exposition, and a clear unfolding of doctrine, more imperative than in what is proudly called our enlightened age; when multiform speculations of strange import are thrust upon the attention of the people; when preaching on taking themes and in the treatment of subjects, seems to aim often at novelty to amuse or startle, rather than substance to instruct; and when vagueness of conception exists painfully in the common mind in regard, often, to some of the first principles of the oracles of God. The consequence to be feared is, that many being less rooted and grounded in principles than those of former times, and being unfurnished with the armor of God, unguarded by the panoply of an intelligent conception of christian doctrine, will not readily detect the specious falsehood and may fall into pernicious errors. It is said, philosophically, that religion is first intuitional and emotional; and after it so exists, it is formulated into a system and becomes theology. The scholar may thus theorize if he please. But, practically, Christianity exists in the great facts of the Bible alone, which are its doctrines, its principles of belief and practice. And personal christianity does not first develop itself from some vague sentiment of natural veneration; it is not a deposit from our own reasonings, which crystalize into christian conviction; but so far as it is christian experience, its very essence is specific truth revealed in the Bible, received into good and honest hearts, and lived in the life. And for this end, instruction in the articles of faith is necessary. Any other religiousness will prove evanescent, unreliable, dangerous. The intuitional and emotional must flow from the Word and keep close to it, or it becomes wild fire; the mother of "all monstrous, all prodigious things," under the name of religion, it may be, but without "fruit unto life eternal." Christians are those who believe in Christ as He is set forth in the

Gospel. And they should be so instructed as to "give a reason of the hope that is in them," because it is a most reasonable thing. Hence, in pastoral work, the importance of doctrinal preaching. "*Go! teach!*" reads the great commission: teach those distinctive principles, doctrines which are the sinews and strength of the christian revelation. Thus will the church become "the pillar and ground of the truth."

But, indeed, it is not our catechisms, which are now discredited, but our very Bibles. Instead of, "In the beginning *God:*" the philosopher now reads; In the beginning, "the potentialities of physical forces." Physical science leads the age; and it is very much in the hands of men manifestly without religious sympathies inclining them "to look through nature up to nature's God;" or men avowedly or covertly hostile to Christianity. It is pure, cold, materialism; anti-supernatural; anti-spiritual; for a large part blank atheism. Yet are their speculations no novelties. The universe came, say they, and was not created. It fell into beautiful, grand, exquisite forms and adaptations, by accident, and not by intelligent design. And, mind, the most wonderful existence of all, evolved itself out of inert, senseless matter; and at the moment of its appearance was as marvellously endowed in the first man as now, and this miraculous power of evolution ended and died. Thus the Bible; our spiritual and immortal being; moral distinctions; God, heaven, hell, are swept away as without authority or utility; and in a very literal and appalling sense, this philosophy proclaims over the departing: "Dust thou art and unto dust thou shalt forever return." Even where such an extreme of atheism is not reached, this same unbelieving spirit cavils at the plain interpretation and authority of the Bible. It is, says the Judas critic, a good book in many respects, but is not in any special sense inspired and infallible. Science discredits many of its representations. It no longer satisfies the reason of the age. And the history and teachings of Jesus Christ, and those of His Apostles, must be received, explained or rejected, as our new light may decide. All idea, however, that the book had a special, supernatural origin, was, in a strict sense, a directly inspired gift of God, more than many other writings, is absurd. And you, theologians and Christians, had better take the kindly warning and not make yourselves ridiculous by insisting upon " old wives' fables." But, again, this boasting is not new. So Porphyry and Celsus proclaimed the overthrow of Christianity in primitive times. So spake the Deists of the sixteenth and seventeenth centuries, and so the French encyclopedists. And, all, singularly enough, with the same assumption and arrogance, and scorn of christian faith, which has ever puffed up the infidel objector, as if his cause were already triumphant and Christianity put to rout. Yet it has survived, and they and their works caused no real impediment to its progress. It lives ; its power over the soul is unabridged ; it is cherished by growing numbers ; but where are they and their confident predictions of its downfall? Not an outpost has been fairly carried, and the citadel yet stands impregnable and defiant. The truth is, there exists in the human soul, implanted by its Maker, a conviction of the supernatural, and of immortality and retribution, which the pride of philosophy may silence in a few, but which, in the mass of human kind, not all the philosophy on earth can extinguish. And also of all the religions which have appeared, (and religion in some form man cannot do without), of all these it is felt that Christianity alone fully meets the case. It rests upon its own proper evidence, both external and within, and is realized to be reasonable, elevating, satisfying, sufficient. His Bible teaches the humble believer a more sensible cosmogony than theirs; his catechism unfolds sublimer truths : to them his best reason assents, and scorns the other. To his Bible, the catechism of his youth, the faith of his fathers, a divine Redeemer and immortal hope through Him, he cleaves, against all the wisdom of the wise—which is foolishness with God. And the best way to foil the unbeliever and confirm the faithful is to keep before the people the direct proofs and doctrines of the Bible; at proper times even by simple catechetical rehearsal. Hence, the wisdom of the church in making some authoritative provision for this end.—The practice of thus keeping the great doctrines of the Bible prominent will also serve to correct another tendency of the times, which is to reduce religion to a mere philanthropy, and of course to confine its range very much to this world and physical wants, rather than to give it its true scope, the life of God in the soul and the life eternal. There is indeed much suffering and sorrow which demand tender sympathy and aid, but which no human power can remove, and which the spiritual power of the Bible alone enables men to support with hopeful submission. And those influences will ever prevent the rebellious suicide from seeking relief by breaking feloniously into the sacred house of life. Poverty and vice, and degradation there are. But they are not to be expelled by closing your Bibles, your churches, your missions, and sabbath schools, and scattering the wealth of the industrious and skillful among the idle or vicious. These evils will always exist, but the only assuaging emollient, the only panacea, is the elevating power of Christianity, as is seen by comparing communities where it operates with those from which it is absent. True religion evermore brings forth the purest and most sustained philanthropy; but philantropy is not all of religion.

I have pointed out our ecclesiastical origin in the established church of Holland. For forty years, the Collegiate was the only church in New Amsterdam. At first, 1626, they worshipped in a large upper room over a horse-mill, which was their house of prayer for seven years. In 1633, at the instigation of Dominie Bogardus, a wooden building was put up near what is now the Old Slip; where they continued to worship until 1642, when a new stone edifice was erected in the fort, at the south-east corner of the Battery, and this they occupied for fifty years, until 1693, when Garden Street was opened—although the location had been seriously opposed as being too far out of town—which objection has also been urged at the erection of each successive new church edifice. Until the erection of Garden Street, the rights of the church and its property had been held by general laws. But in 1696, a regular charter was obtained from the Dutch William, a year or two before that of Trinity. And the names of the consistory chartered are some Dutch, some Huguenot, still found among us. In 1729, the Old Middle, on Cedar and Liberty Streets, long called the New Dutch, and since the Post Office, was dedicated. And in 1769, the North, corner of William and Fulton, then in the fields. Dr. Laidlie preached the dedication sermon, and English preaching was fully established. The old church in the fort was named St. Nicholas, the name of the Dutch tutelary saint, not yet forgotten among those of the true lineage. It has not been in my plan, however, to relate the details of church erections, the lives of the pastors, or minute incidents, occurring through the long history of our ecclesiastical existence. That work has been done by several hands. Much information will be found in Broadhead's *History of New York;* in Dunshee's *History of the School;* in Judge Disosway's volume on *The Early Churches of New York;* and in the sermon of my late revered colleague, Dr. DeWitt, preached at the re-opening of the North Church, in August, 1856. This last is so thorough, as well as authentic in its gatherings, that scarce a few stray sheafs remain wherewith a gleaner may fill his bosom.

With the increase of trade, and for agricultural objects, the colony spread over Manhattan, to Brooklyn, up the river, and into New Jersey; and missions among the Aborigines were also established. It has been claimed that the first Dutch Church was at Fort Nassau or Orange, now Albany. The history of that ancient church is very interesting; but the claim to priority is, I think, without historical foundation. It shows, however, that with the Dutch immigrants, religion went hand-in-hand with commerce. In process of time, after 1664, as the colony grew, other types of worship appeared. But it should be noticed that, with the exception of a few Portuguese Jews who fled to Holland and came here for traffic: and with the exception of the Catholics in Maryland, and also some Spanish Catholic settlements in the extreme South, the whole of eastern North America, now included in the United States, was discovered and settled by Protestants.

And it will remain theirs so long, but only so long, as they are faithful to the trust of civil and religious freedom, extorted from persecuting powers, and confirmed to them as by the last will and testament of the martyrs of the cross: by "the church under the cross," as that of the early Dutch Protestants was significantly named.—In consonance with the example of the mother church, ours has always displayed a catholic spirit in its intercourse with its neighbors: a spirit by no means incompatible with its love for its own fold. When the English took possession, the chaplain of their forces held service by invitation in the church at the Fort, as also did Mr. Vesey, the first rector. When Garden Street was opened the consistory invited him to occupy it part of the day. When he was inducted into the rectorship of Trinity, the English Governor named two of the Dutch ministers to represent the body. On several occasions the consistory has very cordially invited our Episcopal brethren to use our church edifices: and the Episcopal ministers of the olden time on Sabbath evenings attended the Dutch church and sat in the elders' pew, as was the custom with our own ministers. Thus was the good will expressed, that long united England and Holland in ties of mutual advantage and confidence; which was broken from commercial rivalry by Cromwell and the witty and vile Charles II, but which was resumed when William of Orange drove out the Stuarts and bestowed constitutional liberty on England and on America. It has been remarked that social considerations greatly influence the church relations of individuals. And between the Dutch and Episcopalians early intermarriages and the intimate social intercourse they produced, established a very fraternal feeling, which embraced the churches, and which has not yet been lost among their descendants. Indeed, I believe the original Dutch families are now more numerously represented in that body than in our own. In like manner a cordial, friendly feeling and ready co-operation in good works with brethren of other evangelical denominations have always prevailed in the Dutch Church. Yet her spirit was conservative; in doctrine adhering to the Calvinism originally professed; equally removed from Antinomianism on one side and Arminianism on the other; and in practice inculcating not a dogmatical and formal, but spiritual, active piety; believing in true revivals, but opposing the dreams of dreamers and the machinery and excesses of fanaticism. She has been less determined than perhaps she should have been to "enlarge the place of her tents and stretch abroad the curtains of her habitations;" and does not at this day occupy so wide a space as early advantages promised, and as might well be desired. But this fact is by no means to be attributed to her creed or her forms. Many adverse causes have been in operation. Naturally the Dutch are not aggressive; yet they have found on their borders some of the most aggressive and self-reliant people on the face of the globe, who, in settling the New World, have far outstripped them. Again, the persistent use of the Dutch language was very detrimental. The changes also, authorized many years ago when a new constitution was adopted, introduced the idea that she needed greater assimilation to surrounding forms, to make her more popular and give her better vantage ground; and that idea, entirely erroneous as it has appeared to me, has brought forth a brood of innovations, not for her own internal good, nor for the good she was doing and was qualified to do in the general Protestant family and the community at large. The Dutch Church had, by inheritance, a name, a history, an open Bible, a Protestant faith, an earnestness of spiritual life, which gave her the affection and respect of all the Reformed. Her worship was orderly and devout; her customs and usages consonant with propriety and good taste, and were endeared to her people by the tender and sacred associations of childhood and antiquity. The Collegiate Church had its own high position in the city as the Collegiate Dutch Church. And all voices of the past and reasonings toward the future seemed to admonish her with concurrent emphasis, to stand on the old paths and rebuke novelists, and admit only such changes as the change of conditions rendered manifestly imperative. A heedless digging at the roots of an ancient oak may strike and sever those fine fibers that run far down into the soil and give it its nutriment, its leafy glories, its fruit, its long life, and hold it upright and steady in its place. And then a slight wind may shake and lay low the pride of the forest. Yet the old church is not overthrown. Vital power and large resources she has, and wisely directed they will keep her in her proper position of eminence and usefulness. "As a teil tree and as an oak whose substance is (yet) in them when they cast their leaves, so the holy seed is the substance thereof."

The completion of one-quarter of a thousand years brings out an interesting review. The church of the horse-mill has been succeeded by nine church erections, most of them large and imposing structures. Twenty-eight pastors have officiated in the pulpits—five of them still living. Devout men and women in large numbers have filled the seats, formerly in not a few instances, the same pew being occupied by several generations. Nearly twenty-seven thousand children have received baptism. The fifty "Walloons and Dutch," who partook of the first Lord's Supper in that upper loft, have increased to nearly eleven thousand communicants. And of the funds, nearly $400,000 have been given to other churches and ministers, chiefly within the present century. Besides the direct blessings in the conversion of sinners, and in the pure lives, and happy, hopeful deaths of the many pious worshippers, who can compute the indirect influences exerted by such an institution upon the morals, the peace and prosperity of the community? Eternity alone can unroll the record. Would that this memorable day might be to us as that day when the reading of the long forgotten law aroused Israel to remember God's dealings with their fathers, and to covenant anew to walk in his statutes, and observe his ordinances to keep them. Then should our altars glow with fresh flames, and our churches anew would be filled with the divine presence and glory.

I place myself in imagination upon the tongue of Manhattan Island, two hundred and fifty years ago. All nature is clothed in the garments it wore at the creation. The rivers roll quietly on, and the beautiful bay spreads out its waters unruffled, excepting as the canoe of the Indian shoots across its bosom. But gradually the scene changes. The city rises to view and grows, until it becomes the largest of the Western World, the great heart of the continent, sending the strong pulsations of intellectual, commercial, political, social, religious life, to the remotest extremities. North and South and East and West, the vast wildernesses have been cleared away. In place of sparse tribes, who made the forests their hunting grounds, and the streams their fisheries, appear myriads of the most intelligent and enterprising people in the world; hamlets have given place to populous cities, the wigwam to the palace, adorned with all that wealth can buy, or taste can create. Instead of the whoop of the savage that scared the solitude, the roar of machinery and the bustle of untiring industry animates the rivers, the great lakes, the plains; and now, by modern inventions, time and space seem annihilated, and the North speaks to the South, and the voices on the Atlantic are echoed from the Pacific shores. The colonies have passed into the greatest Republic the world has known, which is felt to be a power among nations, an essential factor in the advancement of the race. The whole primeval wilderness teems with civilized men; the wide domain is infused and impelled by the thought and principles of Christianity, and a new continent is set as a brilliant star in the crown of Immanuel.

We turn to the East, and the ocean, over which small shallops brought adventurous men to unknown lands is crossed in every direction by multitudes of ships, carrying the stores of both continents to and fro, and hundreds of thousands of voyagers. Meantime, Europe has more than once been shaken to its foundations and presents a new aspect. Some of the old monarchies survive; but thrones have been cast down; old institutions have vanished; the masses have been elevated; the stately grandeur and arrogance of the few humbles itself before the many, and political forms appear, in which the people are considered as an element in the state. Literature, science, the mechanical arts, have made astonishing progress, and changed the very face of life. Popery and Mohammedanism have lost their significance, and are manifestly hasting to their predicted end. The Oriental world has thrown down its separating walls, and the faith, enterprise, civilization, religion of the west are introducing new ideas, a new faith and new soul into their effete systems. "Eastern Java now kneels with the native of the farthest west and worships." No former period of history, not the rise and supremacy of Imperial Rome when it spread Roman power, and thoughts and institutions over the nations; nor when the empire broke into the ten prophetic kingdoms behind which the little horn came up to seduce, and subdue, and crush all other power; no portion of recorded time has wrought such changes upon man's earthly habitation, and thoughts and modes of living as have occurred during the life-time of this church. The politician and the historian see truly, but see only the effects of man's agency and rest in second causes. The Christian surveys the scene in another spirit, and recognizes the march of the King of Kings "whose goings forth have been from of old, from everlasting." He sees in all the course of time, and especially in these later events, the acts of Jesus Christ whose is this world and who seems now hasting His preparations to take full possession of His purchased Kingdom, "the earth and the fulness thereof." He sees and adores.

But what eye can pierce the darkness; what human sagacity can forecast the events of the next 250 years? It is not given to man to read the future. But the Scriptures utter divine revelations, and say "let him that readeth understand." Upon that darkness, then, we turn the lamp of prophecy, and wondrous scenes are unfolded to the eye of faith. Long before those years shall have run their course the millennial glory, as we believe, shall have overspread the earth. Not in the degradation of the mediator, Christ, to a human shape, surrounding himself with the pageantry and low splendors of a worldly monarchy shall it be. But upon the throne to which He ascended, sitting at the right hand of the Father, "He shall see the travail of His soul;" the life of sorrow; the agony of the garden; the impalement of Calvary; the disgrace of death; His incarnation and atonement in their blessed fruits, "and shall be satisfied." The church shall continue its offices, not, as we believe, all merged in one, but still diverse in form to suit diversity of tastes, yet truly one in mutual recognition, and brotherhood and love. Governments will exist, and they not one, perhaps, but several. Social and civil life will go on as now, for men will still be men, but good men. And learning and the arts of life, inventions and discoveries which even in our day of wonders we can scarce imagine, will be in full operation. Wars and rumors of wars shall be no more heard. Commerce shall interchange the riches of all climes and bring all people into kind fellowship. All these various agencies in harmonious action, which are God's providence over the world, and above all, Christianity, the one acknowledged religion, pervading and animating all hearts, all relations, all duties; these and such shall be the days of the Son of Man on the earth and they shall last a thousand years. Then, and now speedily perhaps, shall be heard the gratulations of a renovated race. The prophetic sea of peoples, and nations and tongues, so long at strife, shall have rocked itself to rest. And diverse languages shall make no discord, but become the several parts in the one hymn of praise; and there shall go up from all peoples and tongues under heaven, earth's grand hallelujah chorus, and the burden shall be: "Now is come salvation and strength, and the Kingdom of our God and the power of His Christ."

Services in the Evening.

These were conducted according to the following programme, which was carried out to the minutest particular.

Programme for Evening Service.

Rev. Talbot W. Chambers, D.D., presiding.

1. **Te Deum** - - - - - Mendelssohn
2. **Prayer** - by Rev. W. J. R. Taylor, D.D. { Of the Reformed Dutch Church }
3. **Hymn 557** - - - - Tune, "Austria"

1. Glorious things of thee are spoken,
    Zion, city of our God ;
   He whose word cannot be broken,
    Formed thee for His own abode :
   On the Rock of Ages founded,
    What can shake thy sure repose ?
   With salvation's walls surrounded,
    Thou mayst smile at all thy foes.

2. See, the streams of living waters,
    Springing from eternal love,
   Well supply thy sons and daughters,
    And all fear of want remove :
   Who can faint, while such a river
    Ever flows their thirst to assuage ?
   Grace, which, like the Lord, the Giver,
    Never fails from age to age.

3. Round each habitation hovering,
    See the cloud and fire appear,
   For a glory and a covering,
    Showing that the Lord is near :
   Thus deriving from their Banner
    Light by night, and shade by day,
   Safe they feed upon the manna
    Which He gives them when they pray.

4. **Address** - by Rev. Morgan Dix, D.D. { Of the Protestant Episcopal Church }
5. **Address** - by Rev. E. P. Rogers, D.D. { Of the Reformed Dutch Church }
6. **Anthem** - "The Heavens are Telling." - Haydn
7. **Address** - by Rev. Howard Crosby, D.D. { Of the Presbyterian Church }
8. **Address** - by Rev. Thomas D. Anderson, D.D. { Of the Baptist Church }

Programme for Evening Service.

9 Hymn 1 - - - - Tune, "Sanctus"

1. Holy, Holy, Holy! Lord God Almighty!
    Early in the morning our songs shall rise to Thee:
    Holy, Holy, Holy! merciful and mighty;
    God in Three Persons, Blessed Trinity!

   Holy, Holy, Holy! all the saints adore Thee,
     Casting down their golden crowns around the glassy sea,
   Cherubim and seraphim falling down before Thee,
     Which wert, and art, and evermore shalt be.

3. Holy, Holy, Holy! Though the darkness hide Thee,
     Though the eye of sinful man Thy glory may not see,
   Only Thou art Holy; there is none beside Thee
     Perfect in power, in love, and purity.

4. Holy, Holy, Holy! Lord God Almighty!
     All Thy works shall praise Thy name, in earth, and sky, and sea:
   Holy, Holy, Holy! merciful and mighty;
     God in Three Persons, Blessed Trinity! Amen.

10 Address - by Rev. O. H. Tiffany, D.D. { Of the Methodist Episcopal Church }

11 Address - by Rev. Richard S. Storrs, D.D. { Of the Congregational Church }

12 Hallelujah Chorus - - - - Handel

13 Doxology - Hymn 574. - Tune, "Old Hundred"

1. From all that dwell below the skies
   Let the Creator's praise arise;
   Let the Redeemer's name be sung
   Through every land, by every tongue.

2. Eternal are Thy mercies, Lord:
   Eternal truth attends Thy word;
   Thy praise shall sound from shore
     to shore
   Till suns shall set and rise no more.

14 Benediction

Music will be under the direction of Dr. S. Austen Pearce.

Mr. W. E. Beames will preside at Organ.

The Addresses.

At half-past seven o'clock the Rev. Dr. Chambers took the chair, and the pulpit was occupied by the other pastors and the officiating clergy, At the close of the preliminary music and devotions, the president said :

"The purpose for which we are gathered this evening is to listen to some words of sympathy and congratulation from brethren representing the different ecclesiastical communions by which we are surrounded. The oldest of them dates its origin back to the English conquest, and came naturally to be called at that time the English church, while we were known as the Dutch church. The speaker this afternoon reminded us of the pleasant relations which then existed between the two bodies. Those relations have continued unchanged from that day to this. There was, at the close of the last century, a ripple of controversy on a doctrinal point between one of the ministers of this church (the Rev. Dr. Wm. Linn), and one of the assistant ministers of Trinity, (the Rev. Dr. BENJAMIN MOORE, afterwards Bishop of the Diocese), and it resulted, as such controversies usually do, in each party being more firmly persuaded of his own opinion; but it was conducted without personalities, without bitterness, and left no sting behind.

"I have the pleasure of introducing to you, as the representative of that church, one whom we honor for his own sake, and for his father's sake, and for the sake of the official position which he occupies: the Rev. Dr. Morgan Dix, Rector of Trinity Church."

DR. DIX'S ADDRESS.

Reverend Fathers of the Consistory of the Collegiate Church, and dear friends and brethren:

In the name of the most high God, whose dominion is an everlasting dominion and His kingdom from generation to generation, under whose protection we are gathered together here, and to whom alone we look as the giver of every good and perfect gift, I bring to you, on this two hundred and fiftieth anniversary, the message of good will and peace. Peace be to you in this your spiritual house; peace be to you in your homes and in your hearts; and love with faith from God the Father and the Lord Jesus Christ; and grace be with all them that love our Lord Jesus Christ in sincerity.

Let me begin by disclaiming for myself the very high honor of occupying the first place among the speakers of this evening. That honor belongs to the office I hold, not to the person who fills it. Every one familiar with our metropolitan history knows that the rector of Trinity Church for the time being would, as a matter of course, be present on this occasion. The corporations which you and I represent are the oldest in the City of New York. The Collegiate Church and Trinity Church have long, long histories, which began when this city was comparatively a mere village, and have run on, side by side, in cloud and sunshine, under the providence of Almighty God. We have always been good friends; through some special perils, common to us both have we been brought in safety; our relations in the earliest days were very intimate; and although those relations no longer exist, yet the mutual honor and regard have not failed. Thus it is meet and right that on this great day of your rejoicing we should see each other face to face, and that I should bring to you a kind word from my people, and in their name, as well as on my own part, wish you health and prosperity.

Changes have come with the growing years to your house; but while we keep this feast the thoughts revert, as by instinct, to the Dutch era of our history and the old Dutch Church. With accuracy have you counted the days back into the past. In 1623 the first permanent agricultural settlement was made in New Netherland, and in 1628, five years later, the first Dutch minister arrived at Manhattan, and began the regular exercise of his ministry. That period of our history is appreciated more and more as time passes on. I was trained from my boyhood to honor and love the good old Dutch forefathers, and to admire their simple, homely ways; the studies of mature years have added force and depth to those first impressions. The latest of our historical writers, in treating of those times, says that "it is plain that under the Dutch rule New York must have been the happiest, though not the most progressive, of the American provinces." "That happiness," he adds, "was due to the simplicity and contentment, the easy-going industry and love of harmless amusement, and to the liberal and kindly spirit which marked the men and their manners." "They worked steadily, governed their households wisely, and persecuted nobody." No wonder that they enjoyed life; no wonder that our restless, pushing, driving, ambitious, and dissatisfied people do not enjoy it. Talk as we may of modern enterprise and progress, they do not always bring happiness; they are apt to banish peace and breed discontent and disgust. The happy days are gone, to return no more till men will moderate and curb their desires, and relish, as of old, a quiet, simple life.

You all know that the first form of Christianity professed in this place was brought hither by the settlers from Holland. Your ancestors did nothing without religion. Hither came the dominies, the schoolmasters, the comforters-of-the-sick, along with the first colonists; and on those humble foundations which they laid was invoked the benediction of Almighty God. You know, also, that the Dutch were a liberal and tolerant people; and that, as a consequence of their generous temper and policy, this island became an asylum for the persecuted and oppressed in adjacent parts. It is one of the brightest features in your history; it explains, perhaps, the cordiality with which your invitation to rejoice with you this evening has been accepted.

But while we, descendants of English Churchmen, thus do honor to the virtues of the Dutch and to the spirit of that form of Christianity which they established here, we may claim credit and commendation for the way in which our ancestors behaved themselves when the first period of the history closed. New Amsterdam was taken; it became New York; and the Church of England was planted where the Classis of Amsterdam had been the supreme and only ecclesiastical authority. But observe how scrupulously the rights of your forefathers were respected. There is nothing like it in history; never did conquerors treat the conquered with such deference and consideration. As far as possible the old customs were preserved; private rights, contracts, inheritances, were scrupulously regarded; and as for the Reformed Dutch Church, it seems to have been treated as a sacred thing. It was more than protected; it was actually established by law by an English governor under English auspices. This was, perhaps, no more than a fair return for the good deeds done by your people. When your turn came to be under the yoke, it was said to you in substance: "You shall still be free ; not one of your old customs shall be changed until you change them yourselves; by us you shall not be meddled with ; keep your places of worship, your flocks, and all you have, in peace." And so, to their old church of St. Nicholas, inside the fort, did your people continue to wend their way in absolute security, though English sentries were at the gates ; and within the walls over which the standard of England waved did the good Dutch dominie speak his mind as freely as ever to his spiritual children ; nor was it until they had finished their devotions and withdrawn that the English chaplain ventured within the same house of worship to read his Office from the Book of Common Prayer. I see in this what does credit to humanity; here be kind consideration, mutual respect, and on both sides a study of the things that make for peace. Nor is it strange that when the Episcopal ministry was at length set up, and my reverend predecessor, William Vesey, had appeared in New York, in deacon's and priest's orders, and having his commission as first rector of Trinity Church, the civil ceremony of induction should have taken place in the new stone church in Garden Street belonging to the Dutch congregation, and that among the subscribing witnesses should have been two of the ministers of your faith. It was on Christmas-day, in the year of our Lord 1697, that he was duly inducted into his office by Governor Benjamin Fletcher; and in the same building, for about three months, until the completion of the church of the English congregation, did your Dominie Selyns and our Rector Vesey officiate alternately, the one in the Dutch language, the other in the English tongue.

It is not only on the religious side, however, that you challenge our respect as a historic body; your church was the pioneer of education in this place. The good old Dutch forefathers believed that the fear of the Lord is the beginning of wisdom; and so wherever they sent the minister they also sent the schoolmaster, that learning might go on abreast with religion, and that religion might give its blessing to learning. When the colony passed under English rule the old system was exactly maintained; with this sole difference, that schoolmasters must get their licenses from the Archbishop of Canterbury instead of the Amsterdam Classis. It is generally acknowledged that the existing system of education in the State of New York owes its origin, in part, to the character, policy, and customs of your predecessors, whose scheme, in its general features, was adopted by the English, and whose influence thus remained active long after the reins of civil power had been taken from their hands.

Of such as these specimens are the other parts of the historical record of your venerable household of faith; and for these good beginnings are you justly held in honor by the intelligent citizens of New York. What has been the history of your denomination, from those early days to our own, you know better than we who are exterior to your fold; but, in observing you, we think that we find among the children many of those qualities and traits which pleased us in the fathers. You have little or nothing to do with sensational religion; you seem a sober-minded, steady-going folk; you do not shock us by exhibitions of unwholesome excitement, nor do you, by your manners or words, rob religion of her dignity, or weaken the habit of reverence in the hearts of the young. It has been my fortune to become acquainted, officially, with some individuals of your number; I am now connected in the same way with others, by duties which bring us frequently together; and in these cases, what was at first a professional acquaintanceship has ultimately taken the higher form of sincere respect and affectionate regard. In particular I recall the venerable form, the benevolent features, of one whom I came to honor and love, and on whose memory I shall ever dwell as that of one who seemed a pattern of Christian virtues—the Rev. Thomas De Witt, whose colleague I was for several years in the fulfillment of an important trust, a man whom it was a help and blessing to know. If he and men like him were fair examples of the result of your principles and the quality of your religion, you cannot be thought to have degenerated, even though in name, and perchance otherwise, changes have passed over your house. To that house I cheerfully bring greeting from our people, assuring you of our good will, and trusting that, as years go on, we may work together, under the providence of the Lord of all, for those ends which shall best promote His glory, the salvation of souls through Christ, and the peace and order of the commonwealth.

At the conclusion of the foregoing address, Dr. Chambers said:

"In the early part of this century, one of the congregations of the Collegiate church separated itself from the main body and became independent. This was the Garden Street church. When its house of worship, then, I think, the oldest in the city, was destroyed by the disastrous fire in 1835, it divided itself into two branches, one remaining in the lower part of the city, the other removing up-town. The last pastor of one of those branches, the Rev. Dr Hutton, honored us with his venerable presence this afternoon, and took part in the services. The present pastor of the other, the Rev. Dr. Rogers, for many years minister at Albany, in the church, of what two centuries ago was called Fort Orange, an organization next in age to our own, has consented to speak to us in the name of the other Dutch churches of the island."

DR. ROGERS'S ADDRESS.

Dear Brethren:

It is a matter of congratulation to myself that the duty assigned me on this occasion is one which does not call for lengthened or elaborate address. I come here as one of the children of the ancient household, visiting the old paternal roof, and bringing the congratulations and good wishes of the family circle to the old folks at home. And it is a pleasant thing that it comes just at this season of the year, when we are to keep our annual thanksgiving service which brings together the scattered children of the household, who come back in so many instances throughout our land to see the spot that gave them birth, to see the parents who brought them into being and reared and cherished them, to thank them for all they did for them in their infancy and youth, and to spend a few hours in sweet family union and communion before they separate again to go back to the work and the warfare of life.

There are many of my brethren here to-night, sir, who might more appropriately, more effectively, and more eloquently discharge the duty which the kindness of your Consistory has assigned to me; but there is not one of them all who can do it with a warmer heart, or with a more true affection, or with a higher appreciation of what the Dutch Church in New York owes to this ancient and venerable body. And yet, sir, I have been in a measure perplexed as to the question of identity and propriety here. Why, as I sat this afternoon and listened to that glowing and eloquent description of the history of the Dutch Church of New York, all it had done, all it was, all that God had enabled it to be and to do, I sat in the most comfortable and pleasant state of mind, thinking that I was part of all that, and that my church, having been for nearly two hundred years one of this circle of churches, was the oldest of them all. I find when I look at that document which called me to my native city, after years of absence, to take a pastoral charge here, that I was called by the elders and deacons of the Reformed Protestant Dutch Church in Garden Street, in the city of New York, to be their pastor; and I learned this afternoon what I knew well before, sir, that that old Garden Street church in the city of New York was the very first of the Dutch churches of this city, and for many years was the oldest church in this connection. And so I began to feel really it was a very indelicate thing for me to take any public part in this service, as I was one of the family, and should rather sit and absorb all these delightful and pleasant things which our friend Dr. Dix has begun by saying, and which these other excellent brethren are to continue to say this evening. And yet it is a fact that seventy-two or seventy-three years ago Garden Street did become independent of this venerable body; and so by a strange transformation—transmigration, I should say—one of the fathers has come to be one of the sons, and I am sent here now to speak for the rest of the children. Well, sir, I am glad to be counted as one of the sons, and to have the honor of speaking in behalf of such a respectable family. Sir, I bring you, then, the congratulations, good wishes, and grateful thanks of the other churches of our faith and name in this great city and vicinity. We honor you; we love you; we are grateful to you; we thank God that we belong to the same family circle, and we are grateful to you, grateful to this church, that for this two hundred and fifty years it has held up on this Island and in this land the banner of Christ with such a firm, true, and loyal grasp, never trailing it before the foe. Many a trumpeter blowing the silver trumpet of the Gospel has ascended your towers during this two hundred and fifty years, but in not a single case has the trumpet given an uncertain sound. The pure faith of God's Word, the faith dear to our fathers, the faith transmitted by them to us, the faith sent across the sea to bear fruit in this Western wilderness, has been upheld by them during all this two hundred and fifty years with a true Christian fidelity and Christian heroism; and the children, speaking in their name, are strengthened in their attachment to this ancient faith and these ancient forms by the noble example of fidelity which this church has set us during all these two hundred and fifty years. No man who has sat under the ministry of those men of God whose portraits grace the room in the rear of this building, at which I wish all this vast assembly could look, for they could not see in any portrait gallery in the earth a nobler set of men—men of God, men of culture, men of scholarship, men of devotion; no man can say that the trumpet has in a solitary case given an uncertain sound, but the truths which, as we heard this afternoon, have been testified to by the sufferings and blood of the fathers in the old land, have been presented by the sons with equal fidelity, and have borne abundant fruit in this new world; and all the children, the thousands and tens of thousands of children that have been trained up in this church have been trained up in the same faith. And if you will remember the history of the men who have been reared up in this church and have gone out in the various walks of life, whose names I might recount here, you would say that their history and character were the natural influence of such a thorough and earnest training.

What shall I say of the men themselves who have stood on these towers and preached this faith? I remember some of them. I shall remember them as long as I live. Take the three men who were the pastors of this church in my childhood, who, as I met them sometimes on the Sabbath arrayed in their canonicals, impressed my youthful imagination more profoundly than it has ever been impressed since those days— take these three men, so unlike and with so much individuality about them, and yet such men of power and of such wonderful character—Knox, Brownlee, and De Witt. If these three men alone were to go down to posterity as the representatives of the ministry of this church, their testimony would be one which never could be gainsaid. It would carry convincing power to the very end of time in behalf of the church which had chosen and sat under the ministry of men like these. So I might speak of the laymen of the church—men who, in the various branches of life, at the bar, ministering to the sick, in the walks of trade and finance, have been men distinguished for integrity, for uprightness, for devoutness, for the fear of God and the love of all that was good in man—such men as Wood, Woodruff, Frelinghuysen, Slosson, Smith, Nelson, Van Nest, Suydam, Sturges, Jeremiah, and Brower—and other men whom I cannot recall at the moment, but whose names are household words in the walks of trade and among the brethren of the bar, and their children and their children's children. The church that has trained up and sent forth such men is certainly entitled to the gratitude of all this community.

And, sir, I feel that we owe a debt of gratitude to this church because she has maintained always the externals of worship, not only in their purity, but in their beauty, in their liberality, and in their propriety. My excellent friend who preceded me alluded to this. Surely something is due of gratitude from the children to the parents who have maintained the house of God in its beauty, in its dignity, and who have kept its pulpit sacredly free, as has so well been said, from anything like sensationalism, anything that ministers to the lower tastes of the populace. I thank God that the Dutch Church has no place in it for sensationalists, and if any ever appear for a time among us, they very soon find that they are in an uncongenial atmosphere, and they gravitate inevitably to their own place. I thank God that our Church has always preserved the order, the decorum and dignity of its pulpit, and the beauty and simplicity of its forms of worship. And I am grateful that it has set an example to all churches respecting caring for the ministry of the Word. Her arrangements for them have always been of the most becoming and liberal character. It was said in regard to a certain distinguished New England divine, many years ago, during his call to a certain prominent pulpit, the committee said: "We hope that if you accept our call, you will trust God to keep you humble: you may trust the church to keep you poor." That has not been the principle of this church. She has never had one standard of spirituality for her dominies and another for her members. She has provided things, not only honest, but liberal in the sight of all men, and as believing in the cardinal principle of God's own word, that the laborer is worthy of his hire. And in that she is entitled to the gratitude of her children, and is an example to all her sisters. But, sir, I must not enlarge; in fact, I feel the time is sacred to the representatives of other churches, and that I, as one of you, have nothing to say except we are glad to come back to our own home to see our parents, and to rejoice in their vigor. Why, they are two hundred and fifty years old, but there is not a wrinkle on their brows. Who would suppose that he who enchanted us so long this afternoon was the senior minister of this church? Why, the church is two hundred and fifty years old; but what is two hundred and fifty years? We are just beginning our work—just beginning our life. May you go on and set us a good example in all those things to which I have referred, steadfast to the truth of God, caring for the order and dignity of God's house, respecting and honoring the faithful ministers of God, training up the children in the fear of the Lord and in the faith of Jesus Christ, and giving largely to benevolent causes, and to assist feeble churches. I might have said much on that score, but your character is too well known to need any enlargement. May the past be prophetic of the future. For whatever may be the signs of the times in regard to denominational prosperity and growth, one thing is certain, the power that this church has exerted, and the prosperity to which it has attained in these two hundred and fifty years, has been due to the fact that its foundation was God's truth, the cross of Christ; and that foundation still stands, and on that foundation in years to come this church, still resting and trusting to the power of God's Spirit, has nothing to fear from the progress of time.

We only hope that when generations and generations still, have passed away, and we who are now the children, fathers, and grandfathers, go down to our graves, others will arise up after us to come up to such convocations as this in days to come, and thank God then that this church lives, has done, is doing, and will do a blessed work for God, for truth, for our country, and for the world.

After the performance of the anthem, " The Heavens are Telling," Dr. Chambers said:

" The next oldest denomination in our city is one closely resembling our own in doctrine, and order, and spirit—one with which we have always held in timate and affectionate correspondence. It will be represented here this evening by one equally distinguished in letters, in the professorial chair, and in the pulpit; one who was born and spent the most of his life in this city, and one peculiarly dear to us as springing from an ancestry which for generations has been honored and loved in our Church. I have the pleasure to introduce to you the Rev. Dr. Howard Crosby."

DR. CROSBY'S ADDRESS.

. The Presbyterian Church most joyfully takes its place in the ranks of those who to-night would honor and congratulate the oldest sister church on the Island of Manhattan. We think we hold a very desirable position, chronologically, in the Protestant family in New York. We look to our older sisters, the Reformed Dutch and Episcopal churches, with an affection that is somewhat tinged with reverence, while we look upon our younger sisters, the Baptist, the Methodist, and the Congregational churches with an equal warmth of affection, but, perhaps, tinged somewhat with a patronizing, or, rather, *matronizing* spirit.

We draw from our older sisters that dignity and conservatism which have always marked them, while we also are able to exhibit some of that plastic adaptedness which so characterizes our younger sisters. We think we stand midway between these for great good to ourselves. And yet, historically, there is one fact concerning us which makes us not a little proud in comparison with them all. If we look for that which constitutes a mark of a church's genuineness, we look for martyrdom, for persecution; and we boast of being the only church in the city of New York that began its career amid the storm of persecution. Let me carry you back, if you are not aware of the story, to a fact in the history of this Island of Manhattan. I touch for a few moments (for only a few moments are given me) on the history of the Presbyterian Church here. Let us go back to the month of January, 1707, a cold January day, and we will take a look into the Governor's house. There never was a Colonial Governor in New York who so completely aped the monarch as Lord Cornbury. He was own cousin to Queen Anne, who was then upon the throne. He was determined to make the colonists understand his relationship to the sovereign; and so he carried a little regal state with him in his gubernatorial home. We come to that Governor's house and see those royally-furnished apartments, and behold the Governor himself covered with gold lace, proud of his dignity, sitting at his dinner-table, and at the table, as invited guests, two very marked men—one especially you would note for his noble bearing, a man who was a scholar; a man of fascinating appearance and manner, but with a broad Scotch dialect. These two guests had but lately arrived in New York, and the Governor, Lord Cornbury, had invited them to visit the regal mansion, there to dine with his lordship. They had accepted the invitation, and before that rousing wood fire and the brass andirons in the big chimney, they were enjoying the repast at the Governor's table. What could be more friendly than that? Four days afterward those two men were languishing in the city jail, and there they spent two long, weary months, at the bidding of that same Governor, their host of four days before. One of those men twenty-five years before had come from Scotland as a Presbyterian minister, first to Barbadoes, and then to the colony of Maryland. That Roman Catholic colony of Maryland, and the Quaker colony of Pennsylvania, and the Baptist colony of Rhode Island, were the only three colonies that opened their doors wide to Christians of all denominations.

The Presbyterians had gone into Maryland and into Pennsylvania; the Synod of Pennsylvania had been established in the year 1706, and the outlying churches of that Synod extended into New Jersey, and even into Long Island. This minister came from Maryland, where he had been stationed, and had done a great and good work, northward to look at the land, to New York and New England, and on his arrival in New York had been so courteously (as we have seen) invited by the Governor to take dinner with him, but on the next day, which was Sunday, in the house of one William Jackson, in Pearl street, this same man preached a sermon, held divine service and baptized a child, while his friend, John

Hampton, also went to Newtown, Long Island, and there preached in the church. For this offence of preaching in a colony where there was not only one established church, but two established churches, the Governor felt that his dignity and the dignity of the Crown was assailed. The men were arrested, and it was two months before they were let out of jail and allowed to give bail for their appearance for trial. Now that was the beginning of the Presbyterian Church in this city. At that time there were but four church buildings in the city. There was the old Garden Street Dutch Church; there was Trinity Church at the head of Wall street, and then two other churches allowed by the government, because the service was conducted in a foreign language, and for the benefit of the foreign exiles—the French church in Pine street, the *Eglise du St. Esprit*, and the Church of the Lutherans, on the site that was afterward covered by the old Grace Church on the corner of Broadway and Rector street. These were the only four churches at that time in the city, and the city extended only to Maiden Lane, except upon the East River shore. And yet, twelve years after that, in 1719, the Presbyterian church-building in Wall street was erected—such a change had come over the public opinion. In 1741 a new phase of Presbyterianism marked the city, and the Presbyterian Church in the country from this reason. The old Scotch and Irish Presbyterians had been mingling largely with Presbyterians from England, Wales, and New England. Those who had come from England, Wales, and New England had rather more liberal views with regard to some practical matters than the old staunch men of Scotland and Ireland, and the opinions began to differ and the preaching to be made much wider, until at last, in 1741, there was a complete division, the old side representing the Scotch and Irish Presbyterianism, who made a great deal of what they called "literature," and on the new side the English, Welsh, and New England members, principally, who made a great deal of personal piety; not that all the personal piety was on their, not that all the literature was on the other side, but these were emphasized especially on the two sides. Then this breach was made, and the Synod of New York was constituted; then came the College of New Jersey as a helper to the new side, first planted at Elizabeth, then at Newark, and then at Princeton. After seventeen years of this separation, in 1758 they came together again. This was the origin of Presbyterianism in this city and in this part of our country.

Now we take great pleasure to-night in recapitulating this history to know that all our course in this city has been hand in hand and heart with heart with this glorious old mother church—the Reformed Dutch Church. We rejoice to know that even while differencees have broken out among ourselves, we have never had any differences with this Church, that we always have honored, and honor still more now than ever before. When we may be accused of now and then harboring some elements of sensation among ourselves, we draw nearer to these conservative brethren and are strengthened; and we believe that one of the designs of Providence in maintaining the Reformed Dutch Church in the city of New York was to help our own Presbyterian Church to walk straightly among you. But I will not enlarge. It is from the bottom of our hearts that we, as Presbyterians, give our congratulations to-night. We like such meetings as these. We like to see all who love the Lord Jesus Christ banded together in one service. We wish we could have them from week to week; we wish that all distinctions might be obliterated except the distinctions between those that love Jesus and those who do not; and we shall be just as glad when Trinity invites us to its two hundred and fiftieth anniversary, and come there and take our part and say our words of congratulation, and rejoice with just as great sincerity as we would for our own two hundred and fiftieth anniversary when that may come.

At the conclusion of Dr. Crosby's address, Dr. Chambers said:

"The brother who is next to address us appears for a denomination which could dispute, and I think with some justice, the claim to the special distinction of martyrdom which has been made by the speaker who has just sat down. The honor of being cradled in persecution does, indeed, belong to the venerable body which he so worthily represents. But twenty years before the occurrence of the incident which Dr. Crosby related to us with so much picturesque vividness, a Baptist minister came to Manhattan Island, and although he was not put in jail, he found it convenient to leave the Island much more quickly than he came. This body of Christians, from whom we are separated by order and discipline, but with whom we are most closely united in substance of doctrine; this body, which is identified with soul liberty and soundness of faith, is represented to us this evening by a brother who has long held an important pastoral charge in this city, and has frequently, in union efforts of prayer and conference, been associated with the ministers of our church, and particularly with the one who last went to his rest, Dr. DeWitt. I have the pleasure to introduce to you the Rev. Thomas D. Anderson, D. D., of the Baptist Church."

DR. ANDERSON'S ADDRESS.

I thank you, Mr. President, for taking away from me the somewhat unpleasant duty of referring to our page of martyrdom.

Beloved Brethren in Christ:

To stand on the rock of Plymouth shore first touched by the foot of the landing Pilgrim; to enter the hall in the old State House at Philadelphia, where, with bold but reverend pens, the Declaration of Independence was signed; to walk around the simple tomb by the side of the Potomac at Mount Vernon, where quietly sleeps the dust of Washington, awakens, by the associations surrounding these inanimate objects, the emotions of every patriotic heart.

To read the very sentences of the "Compact" drawn up in the cabin of the Mayflower, moulding the elements of government beneath the sanction of the Almighty; to dwell on the distinguishing characteristic in the charter of Providence Plantations, according to every man, as a right, religious freedom; to slowly read the lines of the original document of the Constitution of the United States, that blend in indissoluble union personal liberty, state rights, and national sovereignty, we come still nearer, as the communicated thoughts possess the mind, to the sources of those ideas which have given to our people individualism, to our communities order, and strength to our nation. In either case, however, we touch not life—in the former, only the inanimate object, in the latter, impersonal idea. But to-night, in reviewing the rise and progress of Christianity and a Christian civilization on our Island and in our State, our contact is with personal life. One living organization in all its vigor stands before us that has spanned the entire period of two hundred and fifty years, since the planting of the Dutch colony at New Amsterdam until the present evening: We are not called to tread, within our Battery, on the consecrated spot where early stood the church within the fort; nor to decipher the venerable parchments containing the symbols of this ancient body; but we grasp living hands which have been joined to others in unbroken succession from that day to this; we respond to the pulsations of the "eternal life," transmitted through renewed hearts from those first believers in Christ, until they throb against our own in the breasts of these brethren whom we are here convened to greet, and who so generously share with us the inspiration of this memorial hour.

Gathering up the faith and love, the impulses and achievements, the history and prophecy of all these years as they are conserved in this living church only to be put forth again a thousandfold in the multiple forms of Christian activity, have we not, brethren, a beautiful image of the Body of Christ of which He is the Head?

If, of the multitudes which, from the vast population of this metropolis, have come to bid you hail on this quarter-millennial birthday, all are not of your own household of faith, shall it be thought to detract aught from your greatness, because in one external ecclesiastical body they do not all bow at one altar? Conditioned as the mind is in our present imperfect state, with an open Bible in our hands, is it not well that all outward restraint be removed, and the soul be allowed, according to its convictions, to shape its faith and practice beneath no other authority than that of God? Is it not to the honor of a *first* Church that around it others have arisen to emulate its excellence and share its sympathies? Is not the strength of the Collegiate Church greater, sharing, as it does, the spontaneous joy in her prosperity of these sister denominations, which is only less than her own, and aided in her efforts by their fraternal co-operation, than it would be if the monotony of an imposed unity had quenched the generous rivalries of different churches? It may well be considered as an additional wreath of bays around your brow, that Episcopalians and Congregationalists, Presbyterians and Baptists, Reformed and Methodists, ask the privilege of laying their tribute of love and prayer on your altar to-night as a testimony to the oneness in Christ of all believers, which, in your kindly relations to other churches, you have so beautifully illustrated.

I have been selected to represent our denomination, not from any special fitness for the service beyond the possession of a heart most deeply to appreciate it, but because I have the honor to be the pastor of our oldest church in this city, which, now through me in behalf of all of like views, extends its hand of fellowship and of cheer.

Our Church has lived by your side for more than half of your long lifetime, and, therefore, we have a right to speak with some authority when we testify our liking for you. We like your *conservatism*, for amid necessary changes we can have no progress, unless we hold fast that which is good. You hold, doubtless, in your creed some articles from which we dissent. But while you hold them as convictions prayerfully drawn from the Bible, our common standard, we would be, not only ungenerous, but untrue to our most dearly-cherished principles if we withheld our honor from your steadfastness. Still further we honor you, not merely for holding your convictions, but also for maintaining inviolate the order by which provision is made to have them statedly presented to your congregations, that they may be thoroughly furnished for every good work. Against indifferentism and the wayward liberality of the age, we honor your conservatism.

We like your *facile practicalness*. What is to be done seems to meet with all instrumentalities ready at hand, without engrafting on the system questionable and untried devices. Although we are taught to believe that no church has a stauncher order, yet nothing stands in the way of the freest engagement in all true enterprises for the moral and spiritual improvement of men. Indeed, your ecclesiastical system appears to us outsiders never to feel a strain while it gracefully bends to all the requirements of Christian benevolence through all its manifold workings. In this facile comprehensiveness there seems to be a place for every temperament, for every order of talent, and for every grade of ministration.

We honor you above all for that *rich evangelical vein* that runs through the writings of your authors, through the sermons of your preachers, and through all the agencies you use for the advancement of Christ's kingdom. It is this which qualifies the Dutch Church to work so harmoniously in union efforts when those efforts have for their object only the glory of God and the well-being of man. For these things, with others not named, we, as Baptists, honor you. Yet, while frankly expressing our regard, we lay no claim to a monopoly of the esteem which I am sure is held by us in common with the other Christian denominations.

Apparently, casual circumstances often hold within them prophecy and symbol. The church within the fort, provided as one of the earliest resting-places for Jehovah Shammah on this Island, bears to my mind such a significance. Let the fort stand for the State, and the inclosed tabernacle for God with us, and by this piece of heraldry we are taught that the stability of the State is secured only as within her borders God abides. He only is the strong tower, the entrenched citadel into which the nation can resort for safety. Walls, and battlements, and the ocean are a defence only when they offer their homage to Jehovah Jireh. Is the fort the nucleus of the State, through whose openings along the avenues of commerce, population, trade, education, and government she will project her future forces? Along with all these, as from a vital centre, must radiate the influences of Immanuel.

Is it too much to say that by some invisible guide this people have been taught to read the prophecy of the church within the fort, and to follow its teachings along the line of their history? So, at first, they sanctified by worship the beginnings of the State; so they dedicated the commerce of the week to the Lord of the Sabbath, for the earth is the Lord's, and the fulness thereof; so from the fort they accompanied population from the Battery to Garden street, to Liberty street, to Fulton street, to Lafayette Place, to Twenty-ninth street, to Forty-eighth street, flanking their march uptown by chapels, Sunday and industrial schools, and missions on the right and left, that there might be none to say in this crowded city, "No man careth for my soul."

When the language of Manhattan changed, with the government, from the Dutch to the English, the vital spirit of the church within the fort transferred the same glorious Gospel from the sonorous speech of Holland to the English vernacular through the ministries of the sainted Laidlie and Livingston. When trade usurped the dwellings of home, the informing Christianity must not be driven from its central position. It entered the busy mart, and at the hour of high noon, in the heart of traffic, true to this prophecy, the prayer-meeting was enshrined, the Fulton Street Prayer-meeting that has offered up before the Throne the prayers of a world. Ever may this church continue a centre of spiritual power, not alone upon this Island, but throughout this nation. Such is the prophecy whose lessons have been so well learned and followed by the Collegiate Church.

When the State shall have passed away, and instead of this earthly metropolis "the holy city, the new Jerusalem," will come down from God out of heaven, prepared as a bride adorned for her husband, although there will be no commerce, for there shall be no sea; although the gates shall not be closed, for there shall be no night there; although the ministries of relief will be ended, for there shall be no more pain; although the sun and moon shall withdraw their light because of the glory of the Lamb; and although in the midst of this four-squared city, with its walls of jasper, its foundation of precious stones, and its gates of pearl, there shall be no temple; when the assembled multitudes, the one hundred forty and four thousand, with the innumerable company which no man can number, shall hear the voice out of heaven saying, "The tabernacle of God is with men, and He will dwell among them, and they shall be His people, and God Himself shall be with them and be their God," then and there, beloved brethren, shall we behold, with admiring gratitude, the radiant glory of our earthly emblem, "The Church within the Fort."

Here the congregation united in singing Bishop Heber's fine anthem, founded on the *Trisagion,* after which the chairman said:

"The next speaker on the list is from the youngest of the great Protestant communities of our country. It is not much more than a hundred years ago when a Methodist minister landed in this city and set up his banner in the name of the Lord; and when we think of what resulted from that venture, the aggressiveness, the fiery zeal, and the wondrous success which attended the efforts of those brethren, we are reminded of the verse of Bishop Berkeley:

'Time's noblest offspring is the last.'

The brother who has kindly consented to represent that communion on this occasion was the pupil of Durbin and McClintock, and well holds up the banner which they unfurled. I have the pleasure of introducing to you the Rev. Dr. Tiffany, of St. Paul's Methodist Episcopal Church."

DR. TIFFANY'S ADDRESS.

Fathers and Brethren:

At the close of the very interesting and admirable discourse to which we listened this afternoon, when my name was announced in the list of speakers for the evening, a clergyman who sat next to me asked, "And what relations have you to the Dutch Church?" This question I now propose to answer by saying that I belong to a Church which, though one hundred and fifty years younger, has had many similar experiences, and has providentially adopted many of the same methods. I think it may be of interest to you to know some facts which may have hitherto escaped your observation.

The one hundred and forty-three years, from 1623 to 1776, exactly represent the interval between the arrival in this country of your "krank-besoekers" from the Netherlands and our "class-leaders" from Ireland. These men performed similar duties in each church; in the absence of clergymen they visited the sick, read and expounded the Bible, and exhorted men to Christian duty and the activities of a Christian life. Your "krank-besoekers" met in a room over a horse-mill,; our "class-leaders" met in a sail-loft. Last month we celebrated the one hundred and tenth anniversary of the dedication of our first meeting-house in John street, and I felt quite a veneration for our antiquity until I came under the shadow of the two hundred and fiftieth anniversary of the Dutch Church. Though so long an interval separates the organization of our churches, yet I find that history repeats itself, and we have many things in common. Each church was felt to be a necessity, and the abundant fruitage harvested by each justifies the wisdom of its separate existence. Both were born in the throes of a spiritual revival, and both were, in some sense, nursed in persecutions, for the title, "The Church of the Netherlands *under the Cross*," had a meaning in the sixteenth century not unlike that attached to the term "Methodist" in the seventeenth. You took the fields for your pulpits a century before Whitefield and Wesley were compelled to resort to them, by reason of the circumstances which surrounded them. Your hymns of praise and songs of salvation were sung in full voice by the congregation of worshippers long before God raised up Charles Wesley to be the sweet Psalmist of our modern Israel. You have always had authorized, but not obligatory forms for public service. If I read aright the motto on the shield of the old North Church, and "*dando conservat*" is an expression of your financial policy, it is only a more classic expression of the plan of John Wesley, who built chapels and carried on his work by means of "a penny a week and a shilling a quarter" from each member of his societies. Your plan of rotation in the pulpits of the Collegiate Churches we have enlarged into an itinerancy which belts the globe.

But you adopted the Calvinistic interpretation of God's Book, and we the Arminian. You, for reasons clearly set forth this afternoon, largely limited your activities to the neighborhood of your first planting, and have in consequence built up a solid character and a robust conservatism, while we have taken a wider range, are less conservative and sedate, more open to the charge of sensationalism, because we have been more largely moulded by the spirit of the age and the genius of more modern institutions. And so, as we come to-night and sit among you, the youngest of your guests, we offer you our hearty greeting, with genuine appreciation of your steadfast adherence to your principles and an honest admiration of your vigorous age.

The service of to-night, however, impresses me more in its bearing on the future than in its relation to the past, for while, in a just sense, it is the culmination of a period in history, in another it is the opening of a field for prophecy. And as, in your admirable and felicitous introduction, Mr. President, you have spoken of the gentlemen who have preceded me as representatives of olden times and older churches, and of me so kindly as a younger member of a younger church, let me, now that the old men have told the dreams which they have dreamt, tell of the vision which this night suggests. The invitation of the oldest Church to all the younger branches, and the hearty response given to these invitations by the presence of so many notable men from all the churches; the coming together on this platform of so many men who represent so many phases of belief and so many forms of worship, is to me an indication that Christian forces are answering Christ's prayer for the unity of His disciples. It indicates that the days of exclusion and separation are giving way to days of fraternization and brotherhood. Union takes the place of controversy; the theological champions and disputants are retiring within their appropriate spheres, the schools and seminaries; and the churches are ceasing to dispute, and are vieing with each other in love and good works. The controversialist of the former days was the product of an age when a man was mighty according to the thickness of the trees against which he lifted up his axe; he has no more a place for his denunciations, nor an audience for his declamation. In an advanced light men have been able to recognize the hidden good which underlies apparent errors. Beneath the differentials of creeds and formulas there is an integral binding principle of life. As a humanness underlies all the varieties of tribe and race, linking men to God and to each other, so a divineness of consecrated living forms links of union among men of varied creeds; a principle of "natural selection" formulated by Christianity centuries ago, when it constituted fraternal love the test of discipleship, saying: "We know that we have passed from death unto life because we love the brethren."

It may be, Mr. President, that in these past days we have all builded unwisely, even though each one's honest effort has been to reproduce his idea of the pattern shown him in his mountain of communion; each building to exhibit his own interpretation of God's plan. Sometimes, mayhap, we have built over against one another. Sometimes there has been in one hand a sword for destruction, while the other held a trowel for construction; but at best we have erected only individual columns, which, however beautiful in our own eyes, scarcely realize Christ's ideal by which the world was to be convinced. May not these individual pedestals and columns be united by a girder of Christian activity and brotherhood, and surmounted by a dome of Christian thought and scholarship, so that each one's best work shall be found to consist in its being part of an holy temple in the Lord; Jesus Christ himself being the chief corner-stone on which the apostles and prophets have built as a foundation?

We heard this afternoon the wonderful announcement "that a rigid Calvinist would not invalidate his orthodoxy if he believed that an Arminian might be saved." After this prodigious step in advance, is it unreasonable to hope for a day when, if the wolf and the lamb may not actually dwell together, and the leopard lie down with the kid, and the calf and the young lion and the fatling together, yet an Arminian and a Calvinist may walk arm in arm, and be closely followed by priest with presbyter, and the procession be enlarged by two agreeing bishops, though one of them may have received his office by the holding up of hands in election, and the other by the laying on of hands in consecration; and all these be seeking for some gathering, be it conference, convention, council, consistory, synod, classis, or assembly, where the only shibboleth for admission shall be "supreme love to God, and corresponding love to the brethren."

And now Mr. President, so far as I may presume to represent the Church of which I am a member, I say, in the language of one of old: "The Lord God of your fathers make you a thousand times so many more as ye are, and bless you, as He hath promised you."

When Dr. Tiffany had concluded, Dr. Chambers said:

"The last speaker on our programme belongs to a body which is at once the oldest and the youngest. It is the oldest, because in New England its origin was coeval with our own, and yet the youngest, because it was within the present century, indeed, some distance in it, that it made a permanent lodgment upon this Island. The relations between the Dutch Church and the Congregationalists have not always been pleasant. Whoever reads the history of the first hundred or hundred and fifty years after the settlement at Plymouth and on this Island will see records of questions which were sometimes very ardently prosecuted as to conflicting jurisdiction; and I remember to have heard the story which, no doubt, is authentic, that a gigantic rooster, such as used to be placed upon the top of the steeples of our churches down in the Fort, was always found pointing, no matter from which direction the wind came, toward the East. It scented danger from that quarter. But these are reminiscences of the past. We bring them up to smile at them. Now, cordiality, friendliness, mutual regard, the strongest desire for each other's welfare and co-operation in efforts for that one cause to which we are all sworn, bind us closely together. The brother who is to speak to us needs no introduction. Although his residence is beyond the East River, and another city claims him as its ornament, yet so often have audiences in New York as numerous as this, and more so, been chained by his words of eloquence and wisdom, that I need only mention his name, the Rev. Richard S. Storrs, D.D., of the Congregational Church, whom I now have the pleasure to introduce."

REV. DR. STORRS'S ADDRESS.

My Christian Friends:

It is not, I think, altogether to the discredit of the Congregational communion, that it has been planted in this great city more recently than the others, the representatives of which have spoken to us so eloquently this evening. Dr. Chambers was mistaken, I am sure, in the inference which he naturally drew from the attitude of that historical rooster. He was up there looking out for recruits! Our churches, at Plymouth, if not at Salem, began earlier than yours, but for centuries Congregationalism was so interested in the progress and success of other communions that whenever it sent any of its representatives to New York, it sent them under a sort of implicit pledge to become either Dutchmen or Presbyterians. Our friend Dr. Bethune used to say—did say once, certainly, in commenting upon a speech from some one who, as he thought, had unduly exalted his own denomination—that he felt bound in justice to his own Church to declare that he presumed that in heaven all Christians would be Reformed Dutchmen. How it may be in heaven I do not know, but a great many Congregational Christians have come to be Reformed Dutchmen when they came to New York. When you have had a promising young man born and bred here, of whom you wanted to make a pillar and an ornament in the Church, you sent him to New England. We Congregationalists have taken him and put him in one of our churches, for five or six years, and then sent him back to you to do grand service, by eloquence and by character: like your venerable senior pastor, Dr. Vermilye. We did the same thing with Dr. Rogers; and if you have got any more such young men, send them along, and we will fit them for your Collegiate pulpits!

It is very delightful to me, my Friends, to stand here this evening, if only to renew the associations of my heart with those men whom I have known, and honored, and loved, in the pulpits of this Collegiate Church, and in the other pulpits of the same communion in this city, with whom in my earlier or later ministry I was familiar, who have passed now into the heavens. I remember well those men to whom reference has been made—Dr. Knox, Dr. Brownlee, and Dr. DeWitt, clear and venerable names! Dr. Milledoler had not ceased from his labor upon the earth, though he had closed his ministry; I remember him as graceful and beautiful, Dr. Brodhead as majestic and charming, in old age. Dr. Dwight of the First Dutch Church of Brooklyn, the successor of Polhemus and Selyns, officiated in an important service at my installation in my church there, thirty-two years ago this week. I never think without fond remembrance of his beautiful face, of his courtesy of manner, of his tender interest in all good men and good things, and of the prayer on which that evening he lifted us all toward the heavens. And the wit, the poet, the accomplished scholar, the careful theologian, the eloquent orator, the devout and adoring Christian, Dr. Bethune, whose funeral I attended in this very church sixteen years ago, was for years my nearest neighbor, almost, and among my most intimate friends. I cannot but think if he were here to-night, to utter his kindling and lofty thought, in his impassioned eloquence, with his voice that spoke like a harp and rung like a trumpet—if he were here to-night, to utter his love and veneration for the Church to which his manhood and his age had been given, and in which his heart was garnered up, how silent our lips would be! and how our hearts would throb within us!

These have gone into the heavens. Ah! yes, but they are the representatives to us, let us not forget, of all who have ascended with them, in the history of this Church for two hundred and fifty years. Back to the forest and the swamp, back to the days of the tomahawk and the Indian bow, of the wampum and the birch canoe, this history carries us. How many have gone up, through the ministry of truth here, rising on the wings of prayer and adoration on earth, and then rising with the angelic cohorts in the heavens, whose thought may be with us to-night! The mountains are full of the radiant presence. More are they that have ascended than they who tarry. The greater, the nobler, and the lovelier company is on high. Ah! my Friends, the church on earth and that above but one communion make; and it is beautiful to stand here, in that communion, and to feel ourselves surrounded and over-watched by this great cloud of witnesses, by this celestial company!

Two hundred and fifty years. Yet, as I have sat here this evening, I have been thinking, my Friends, how small a part of the real history that is! How the roots of this history run back, far beyond that, into a grand and heroic preceding age. The history of the Church in Holland, of which this was here the earliest representative, is the most illustrious and sublime history of modern Europe. The communion with which I have been associated, in all my public life, sprang from a parallel movement in England, but it never was marked by the same heroic endurance, the same frequent sacrifice unto martyrdom, which was familiar in the Church in Holland. I remember what the historian tells us, of the 18,000 whom Alva burned or butchered or buried alive, to trample out the Reformed religion in the Netherlands. I remember the massacres at Antwerp, at Naarden; and I say again that there is no page in the history of modern Europe so magnificent as that.

It was true of the Dutch Church, as it has somewhere been said of Christianity itself, that it sprang up under the axe, it flourished in the blast, and it blossomed in the flame. It had a grand renown, back of New Amsterdam, back of this continent, and of the ocean before us. You trace your lineage to the most royal workers and champions of the truth in modern times. No wonder you cherish that magnificent renown! It is a sublime inheritance. And standing here to-night, with the thought which the last brother has suggested, that this occasion looks forward as well as backward, we certainly, representatives of other communions, can ask for you no greater blessing, no richer endowment of God, than that the same sublime qualities which were illustrated in that history may continue in you and in your children to the end of time—the same constancy of faith, the same sovereign devotion, in the gospel of God.

We have heard to-night, and it has been truly said, that this Church has been conservative of the truth. It could not have been otherwise, without being supremely unfaithful to its illustrious history. It was not a gospel of "mush" and nonsense for which men met death with untrembling hearts, and women submitted to be buried alive. It was a gospel with not one prophecy too many, pointing forward to the coming of the Lord, with not one miracle too many, to illustrate His divine power and supremacy—a gospel in which was the offer of forgiveness through the atonement, and of purification by the Holy Ghost, and a heavenly promise for those who received it.

Carry on that gospel, so majestic, and glorious, and divine, appealing so powerfully and vividly to the faith of the fathers, into your subsequent history as a church; and it shall be the power of God, upon you and with you, for all the centuries! Carry on, as well, their spirit of self-sacrifice.

Churches grow by self-consecration. That motto I remember which Dr. Tiffany has referred to—"*dando conservat:*" the church stands and grows by giving. The church comes to be what it ought to be by communicating. The fervent missionary zeal of the Church in Holland was one great secret of its magnificent rise and power. Men like your missionaries, Scudder, Abeel, beloved disciples, going to carry the gospel to the heathen on distant shores, are working for your enlargement, for your permanent continuance, as truly and as effectively as though they were at home.

Carry on the same spirit which was in the fathers, of love for liberty and for learning. We remember that splendid example given by the citizens of Leyden, when after their heroic endurance of the siege, in reward or recompense of their valor and patience, they were permitted to take their choice between the remission of a certain heavy and perpetual tax, or the establishment of a University. Now, I don't know, I won't undertake to say, what the citizens of New York would do if such a proposition were made to them; but the citizens of Leyden, hunger-bitten, famine-stricken, staggering in their wan and wasted frames along the streets that had been smitten as by the blast of fire in that terrific siege, chose the University. All honor to the memory of their wisdom and nobleness! I remember, too, that in the hall, I think, of the University at Utrecht, around the dome were placed or planned words which declared that "the seat of learning is the natural cradle of liberty."

Yes, it is true that the hall of human wisdom has been the cradle of liberty, there and elsewhere. It is for us joyfully to remember that the Declaration of Independence, written by our fathers, caught its spirit, and even its terms, in part, from the Declaration of Independence signed at the Hague in 1581; and that the union of the American colonies followed closely the example of the union of Utrecht, which was the corner-stone of the Netherland Republic.

As long as this sovereign constancy to the gospel, as long as this sublime spirit of consecration, fortitude, and self-sacrifice, as long as this love of learning and of liberty combined, remain in the Dutch Church, its future is secure. Wealthy or poor, numerous or few, that makes no difference. The church which has these elements within it, and which does its work in the inspiration of them, is the Church of the Future in America.

Two hundred and fifty years! How utterly incredible, how inconceivable, this city would have seemed to those who founded this church in its feebleness two hundred and fifty years ago, looking out from the fort of which Dr. Anderson has told us; seeing in prophetic vision these vast avenues, these populous squares, these thundering trains along the streets—this city sweeping upward and outward, eastward, northward, westward, and on every hand, and already beating with the tread of millions of feet—incredible, indeed! They could not have conceived it. How little can you and I conceive what this city is to be, two hundred and fifty years in the future! what millions of population are to be gathered in it! how its piers are to throb with the commerce of the world, crowding against them! how its influences are to go out over all the land, and to the ends of the earth! The same faith in the gospel, the same constancy, fidelity, and self-sacrifice, the same love for liberty and for learning, and the same hospitality toward other communions, which were the glory of this Church in its earlier life, and have been ever since, will give to that city of the Future influences that shall keep it pure and make it purer, and will give to the semi-millennial anniversary of this Church a glory that we cannot prefigure, and can only vaguely anticipate. God grant it!

I remember the inscription on the monument of the great Admiral Van Tromp, in the old church at Delft, written in Latin, the close of which may, perhaps, be not unfairly translated thus: "At last, in battle with the English, himself unconquered, if not the victor, he ceased at the same moment to triumph and to live." I hope that the epitaph of this Dutch Church never will be written, while the continent stands; but when it is written, or spoken, in the last consummation, when the Lord himself appears in the air, I trust it may be said, and truly said of it, that if not itself the conqueror over all forms of sin, it was itself unconquered, and that it ceased to triumph for the Master only when it ceased to live!

The Succession of Pastors.

1628—1878.

JONAS MICHAELIUS, (circa.)	1628–1633
EVERARDUS BOGARDUS,	1633–1647
JOHANNES BACKERUS,	1647–1649
JOANNES MEGAPOLENSIS,	1649–1669
SAMUEL MEGAPOLENSIS,	1664–1668
WILHELMUS VAN NIEWENHUYSEN,	1671–1682
HENRICUS SELYNS,	1682–1701
GUALTERUS DU BOIS,	1699–1751
HENRICUS BOEL,	1713–1754
JOANNES RITZEMA,	1744–1784
LAMBERTUS DE RONDE,	1751–1784
ARCHIBALD LAIDLIE,	1764–1779
JOHN HENRY LIVINGSTON,	1770–1812
WILLIAM LINN,	1785–1805
GERARDUS ARENSE KUYPERS,	1789–1833
JOHN NEILSON ABEEL,	1795–1812
JOHN SCHUREMAN,	1809–1811
JACOB BRODHEAD,	1809–1813
PHILIP MILLEDOLER,	1813–1825
JOHN KNOX,	1816–1858
PASCHAL NELSON STRONG,	1816–1825
WILLIAM CRAIG BROWNLEE,	1826–1860
THOMAS DE WITT,	1827–1874
THOMAS EDWARD VERMILYE,	1839——
TALBOT WILSON CHAMBERS,	1849——
JOSEPH TUTHILL DURYEA,	1862–1867
JAMES MEEKER LUDLOW,	1868–1877
WILLIAM ORMISTON,	1870——

The ensuing Stanzas, from the fertile and graceful pen of William Oland Bourne, Esq., are taken from the columns of the "Christian Intelligencer," of the week following the celebration:

Hymn.

Suggested by the Two Hundred and Fiftieth Anniversary of the Collegiate Church, City of New York, Thursday, November 21st, 1878.

God of our Fathers! Thee we praise!
   Eternal King! our sovereign Lord!
For all Thy love our songs we raise,
   Forever be Thy name adored.

Through changing years, and scenes that pass
   Like shadows on the path of time,
Thy mercies all our praise surpass,
   Enduring as Thy truth sublime.

The promise spoken by Thy Son,
   Thy saints in holy trust believed,
In tears and blood their course they run
   Till they the conqueror's crown received.

"Lo! I am with you to the end!"
   We praise Thee for the Word divine;
Give grace, O Lord! all hearts to blend
   In love to this dear Church of Thine.

Give to this Zion life and light!
   Build up its walls and altars strong!
Till all its love and labor bright
   Shall end in Heaven's eternal song.

Note.

The following diagram accurately represents the lettering upon the top of the Memorial Cane, presented on the day of the commemoration to the Senior Pastor, by A. V. W. Van Vechten, Esq., as noticed in the prefatory remarks by Dr. Vermilye.

www.ingramcontent.com/pod-product-compliance
Lightning Source LLC
Chambersburg PA
CBHW021919180426
43199CB00032B/1042